greatest ever

one pot

p

This is a Parragon Publishing Book
First published in 2004

Parragon Publishing
Queen Street House
4 Queen Street
Bath BA1 1HE, UK

ISBN: 1-40543-119-9

Printed in Indonesia

Produced by the Bridgewater Book Company Ltd.

NOTE

This book uses metric and imperial measurements. Follow the same units
of measurement throughout; do not mix metric and imperial.
All spoon measurements are level: teaspoons are assumed to be 5 ml,
and tablespoons are assumed to be 15 ml. Unless otherwise stated,
milk is assumed to be full fat, eggs and individual vegetables such as potatoes
are medium, and pepper is freshly ground black pepper.

The times given for each recipe are an approximate guide only
because the cooking times may vary as a result of the types of oven
and other equipment used.

Recipes using raw or very lightly cooked eggs should be
avoided by infants, the elderly, pregnant women, convalescents and anyone
suffering from an illness. Pregnant and breast-feeding women
are advised to avoid eating peanuts and peanut products.

Contents

Introduction

Preparing food at home can give you a great sense of satisfaction, but it can seem something of a chore, and clearing up afterward is often very tedious. If you have a busy life, one-pot meals may well be exactly what you need. Cook meals in batches and freeze, then heat in the  microwave when you need them and relax for a few minutes. Running a household, holding down a job, and feeding the family can be difficult to balance, and one-pot meals are the ideal time-saving solution. They make busy lives easier, and generally make less mess in the kitchen. Most of the recipes in this book are cooked in a single pot; the remainder involve more complex preparation but all finished dishes end up in a single pot.

Most one-pot dishes can be served straight from the cooking pot, avoiding the need for multiple serving dishes. If you are going to be entertaining friends with these recipes, it is a good idea to find a set of casseroles that look great when you serve from them at the table. One more advantage is that the food is kept piping hot, which saves you having to warm plates in the oven.

Making the most of one-pot dishes

An easy way to make the most of one-pot dishes is to serve them with a side salad of pasta or rice, or the more conventional lettuce, cucumber, and tomato. You can change the taste of a whole meal by adding a salad dressing, either just before you serve, as a garnish, or at the table. Try strongly flavored salad dressings, such as blue cheese, with meat dishes; and lighter dressings, such as vinaigrette, with chicken and risottos.

Experiment with adding more unusual ingredients to salads, such as fruit, nuts, croutons, or lardons. Segments of orange add a lovely tangy flavor, as well as a splash of color. Try adding fruit to a salad when serving with meat that traditionally goes well with fruit, such as duck or pork. Pine nuts, especially if they are toasted, make a quick and attractive addition and will not overwhelm the flavor of anything else. Croutons are often flavored with garlic

and/or herbs and are best added to a salad served with a strongly flavored dish. Add them just before serving, otherwise they tend to go soggy. If croutons in your pantry go stale, sprinkle them with a little milk and spread out on a baking sheet, then bake in a preheated oven, 425°F/220°C, for a few minutes, or until crispy again—serve at once. Ready-made lardons and croutons are available in most supermarkets, and will retain all their flavor and crispness as long as they are stored adequately.

Nowadays, many unusual and exotic types of salad greens are available. Experiment with their different flavors, colors, and textures. Try salads made with arugula, oak leaf, radicchio, mizuna, and tatsoi, or combine these with more conventional leaves, such as romaine, Boston, and iceberg, and more conventional ingredients, such as tomatoes, radishes, and beet for color, and scallions, shredded cabbage, and anchovies for flavor. Baby spinach leaves also make good salads. Look at your pantry standbys for inspiration—try adding tuna, capers, a drizzle of balsamic vinegar, and/or freshly grated Parmesan cheese.

Fresh herbs are a simple and attractive addition to salads. Try adding dill to a potato-based salad or a salad served with fish. A drizzle of olive oil and a handful of fresh, chopped herbs are all that is needed for many salads—snipped chives are an excellent addition.

You can make your own salads of delicatessen quality at home, as well as plain lettuce and tomato salads. Pasta salad and rice salad can be made as a one-pot dish. Add any fresh vegetables that you have in the refrigerator— bell peppers, diced cucumber, bean sprouts, grated carrot— and you can also add hard-cooked eggs, peanuts, sunflower seeds, or cubes of cheese. You can make it up as you go along, and this can be one of the most enjoyable ways of preparing a meal. You can use potatoes and beans as a basis for salads, too. Mixed bean salad is delicious made with red kidney beans, cannellini beans, and great Northern beans, and is quick and easy to prepare. You can base your salad around any ingredients; try tomato salad with onions or coleslaw with golden raisins.

Many salad dressings can easily be made at home and will keep quite well in the refrigerator. Their flavor will be superior to the store-bought versions, and you can eliminate the need for colorings, additives, and preservatives. You can easily add a handful of chopped fresh herbs or other ingredients to a plain mayonnaise to adapt it to the dish you are serving. Try adding a handful of crumbled blue cheese, such as Stilton, to a plain mayonnaise and then beat well, to make a strong and delicious accompaniment to stews and casseroles. Add freshly snipped chives or dill for a salad dressing, which will complement chicken, potatoes, or fish. You can add anything —try sun-dried tomato or garlic oil in a dressing in place of the plain oil.

Bread is also a great accompaniment to most one-pot dishes, and can be served with or instead of a salad. Slices of basic white bread can be used for mopping up juices from stews, soups, and casseroles, but many different and more interesting breads are now available. Most freeze well, and will keep for up to three months in the freezer. Remove and let stand at room temperature for about 24 hours before serving.

Most supermarkets and some smaller stores now have quite an extensive range of French bread, Italian bread,

and other more exotic breads. French bread is delicious served with soups, is inexpensive, and looks attractive. Serve fresh and warm, if possible, with lots of butter and a side salad. Ciabatta and focaccia are Italian breads, most often baked with herbs. Both of these are ideal for serving with one-pot dishes with a lot of liquid, especially soups and stews. Improvise with bread that is available in stores, or bake it at home. Freeze a few different types of bread if your store has a good selection.

You can make an easy cheat's garlic bread by buying hot, fresh French bread if you live near a baker's. Make some garlic butter using soft, warm butter, a little garlic, herbs, and salt and pepper. Make vertical slits along the length of the bread with a knife, then spread a little of the butter inside the slits. Make sure the bread and butter are warm and that you use only a little garlic—it will taste stronger because it has not been cooked.

A simple way to liven up stews and casseroles and make them more substantial is to top them with bread and cheese. French bread works particularly well, but you can use any bread that can be cut into thick slices. This is a great way to use up stale bread, as it works better than fresh bread. Cut the loaf into thick rounds or slices and spread with a thin layer of butter or olive oil. Thinly slice some cheese— Cheddar, Edam, and Gruyère all work well—and place some on top of each slice of bread. Toward the end of cooking, place the slices of bread and cheese on top of the casserole so that the bottom of the bread absorbs a little of the sauce and the cheese on top melts. Depending on your tastes, you may like to try placing a slice of tomato between the bread and cheese before cooking. If you are going to use oil instead of butter, a spray canister of oil ensures that you do not use too much. Alternatively, you could simply place a slice of bread and cheese in the base of each individual soup bowl before ladling in the hot soup or stew.

If you are making a one-pot soup and it looks too weak, try adding some pâté to thicken it and add some more flavor. This works best with strongly flavored soups, such as tomato, beef, and lentil.

To add an attractive garnish to bowls of tomato soup and other dark-colored soups, place a small spoonful of cream in the center and run a toothpick through it to make a swirl. Sour cream or plain yogurt add a creamy texture and flavor to soups, and should be added toward the end of the cooking time to heat through.

Meat

From ham to sausages and from beef to pork, you are sure to find an easy-to-prepare midweek supper or something special to serve guests. This chapter is packed with great ideas for meaty soups, succulent stews, spicy curries, and almost-instant stir-fries. It includes familiar favorites, such as Scotch Broth (see page 10) and Chili con Carne (see page 34), and classic dishes, such as Pork Stroganoff (see page 42) and Lamb Biryani (see page 59). Adventurous cooks will enjoy experimenting with more unusual meats, trying out such recipes as Maltese Rabbit with Fennel (see page 36). There are meals with child appeal, luxurious special-occasion dishes, hearty winter warmers, tasty light lunches, hot or aromatic curries, and recipes from countries as far apart as China, Mexico, and Italy. In fact, something to suit all tastes—just popped into the pot.

scotch broth

generous ¼ cup pearl barley

10½ oz/300 g lean boneless lamb,
such as shoulder or neck fillet,
trimmed of fat and cut into
½-inch/1-cm cubes

3 cups water

2 garlic cloves, finely chopped
or crushed

4 cups chicken or meat stock

1 onion, finely chopped

1 bay leaf

1 large leek, cut into fourths
lengthwise and sliced

2 large carrots, finely diced

1 parsnip, finely diced

4½ oz/125 g rutabaga, diced

salt and pepper

2 tbsp chopped fresh parsley

1 Rinse the pearl barley under
cold running water. Put in a pan
and cover generously with water.
Bring to a boil and boil for 3 minutes,
skimming off the scum from the
surface. Set aside, covered, in the pan.

2 Put the lamb in a large pan
with the water and bring to a
boil. Skim off the scum that rises to
the surface.

3 Stir in the garlic, stock, onion, and
bay leaf. Reduce the heat and let
simmer very gently, partially covered,
for 15 minutes.

4 Drain the pearl barley and
add to the soup. Add the leek,
carrots, parsnip, and rutabaga.
Continue simmering for 1 hour, or until
the lamb and vegetables are tender,
stirring occasionally.

5 Taste and adjust the seasoning.
Stir in the parsley and ladle into
warmed bowls to serve.

COOK'S TIP

Trimming the lamb cuts the fat
content of this soup. By making
it ahead, you can remove any
hardened fat before reheating.
This traditional winter soup is
full of goodness, with lots of
tasty golden vegetables along
with tender barley and lamb.

cabbage soup with sausage

12 oz/350 g lean sausages,
preferably highly seasoned

2 tsp oil

1 onion, finely chopped

1 leek, halved lengthwise and
thinly sliced

2 carrots, halved and thinly sliced

14 oz/400 g canned chopped
tomatoes

12 oz/350 g young green cabbage,
cored and coarsely shredded

1–2 garlic cloves, finely chopped

pinch of dried thyme

generous 6⅓ cups chicken or
meat stock

salt and pepper

freshly grated Parmesan cheese,
to serve

VARIATION

If you don't have fresh stock
available, use water instead,
with only 1 bouillon cube
dissolved in it. Add a little more
onion and garlic, plus a bouquet
garni (remove it before serving).

1 Put the sausages in water to cover generously and bring to a boil. Reduce the heat and let simmer until firm. Drain the sausages. When cool enough to handle, remove the skins, if wished, and thinly slice.

2 Heat the oil in a large pan over medium heat, then add the onion, leek, and carrots and cook for 3–4 minutes, stirring frequently, until the onion starts to soften.

3 Add the tomatoes, cabbage, garlic, thyme, stock, and sausages. Bring to a boil, then reduce the heat to low and cook gently, partially covered, for 40 minutes, or until the vegetables are tender.

4 Taste the soup and adjust the seasoning, if necessary. Ladle into warmed bowls and serve with Parmesan cheese.

winter beef & vegetable soup

serves four

generous ¼ cup pearl barley, rinsed

5 cups beef stock

1 tsp dried mixed herbs

8 oz/225 g lean rump or sirloin beef

1 large carrot, diced

1 leek, shredded

1 onion, chopped

2 celery stalks, sliced

salt and pepper

2 tbsp chopped fresh parsley,
    to garnish

crusty bread, to serve

VARIATION

This soup is just as delicious
made with lean lamb or pork
fillet. A vegetarian version can be
made by omitting the beef and
beef stock and using vegetable
stock instead. Just before
serving, stir in 6 oz/175 g firm
tofu, drained and diced. An even
more substantial soup can be
made by adding other root
vegetables, such as rutabaga
or turnip, instead of, or as well
as, the carrot.

1 Place the pearl barley in a large
pan. Pour over the stock and add
the herbs. Bring to a boil, then cover
and let simmer for 10 minutes.

2 Meanwhile, trim any fat from
the beef and cut the meat into
thin strips.

3 Skim away any scum that has
risen to the top of the stock with
a slotted spoon.

4 Add the beef, carrot, leek, onion,
and celery to the pan. Return to a
boil, then reduce the heat, cover, and
let simmer for 20 minutes, or until the
meat and vegetables are just tender.

5 Skim away any remaining scum
that has risen to the top of the
soup with a slotted spoon. Blot the
surface with paper towels to remove
any fat. Adjust the seasoning according
to taste.

6 Ladle the soup into warmed
bowls and sprinkle with parsley.
Serve accompanied by crusty bread.

beef & vegetable soup

serves four–six

8 oz/225 g tomatoes

2 ears fresh corn

1 carrot, thinly sliced

1 onion, chopped

1–2 small waxy potatoes, diced

¼ cabbage, thinly sliced

4 cups beef stock

¼ tsp ground cumin

¼ tsp mild chili powder

¼ tsp paprika

8 oz/225 g cooked beef, cut into
   bite-size pieces

3–4 tbsp chopped cilantro (optional)

hot salsa, to serve

1 To peel the tomatoes, place in a heatproof bowl, then pour boiling water over to cover and let stand for 30 seconds. Drain and plunge into cold water. The skins will then slide off easily. Chop the tomatoes.

2 Using a large, sharp knife, cut the ears of fresh corn into 1-inch/ 2.5-cm pieces.

3 Place the tomatoes, carrot, onion, potatoes, cabbage, and stock in a large, heavy-bottom pan. Bring to a boil, then reduce the heat and let simmer for 10–15 minutes, or until the vegetables are tender.

4 Add the corn pieces, the cumin, chili powder, paprika, and beef pieces. Return to a boil over medium heat.

5 Ladle into soup bowls and serve sprinkled with cilantro, if using, with salsa handed round separately.

COOK'S TIP

To thicken the soup and give it a flavor of the popular Mexican steamed dumplings known as a tamale, add a few tablespoons of masa harina (whole ground white or yellow corn), mixed into a thinnish paste with a little water, to the corn, spices, and beef. Stir well, then cook until thickened.

beef, water chestnut & rice soup

serves four

12 oz/350 g lean beef, such as
rump or sirloin

4 cups beef stock

1 cinnamon stick, broken

2 star anise

2 tbsp dark soy sauce

2 tbsp dry sherry

3 tbsp tomato paste

4 oz/115 g canned water chestnuts,
drained and sliced

2½ cups cooked white rice

1 tsp grated orange rind

6 tbsp orange juice

salt and pepper

TO GARNISH

strips of orange rind

2 tbsp snipped fresh chives

VARIATION

Omit the rice for a lighter soup
that is an ideal appetizer for an
Asian meal of many courses. For
a more substantial soup that
would be a meal in its own right,
add diced vegetables such as
carrot, bell pepper, or zucchini.

1 Carefully trim away any fat from the beef. Cut the beef into thin strips and then place in a large pan.

2 Pour over the stock and add the cinnamon, star anise, soy sauce, sherry, tomato paste, and water chestnuts. Bring to a boil, skimming away any surface scum with a slotted spoon. Cover the pan and let simmer gently for 20 minutes, or until the beef is tender.

3 Skim the soup with a slotted spoon again to remove any scum. Remove and discard the cinnamon and star anise and blot the surface with paper towels to remove any fat.

4 Stir in the rice, orange rind, and juice. Adjust the seasoning if necessary. Heat through for 2–3 minutes before ladling into warmed bowls. Serve garnished with strips of orange rind and snipped fresh chives.

chunky potato & beef soup

serves four

2 tbsp vegetable oil

8 oz/225 g lean rump steak,
    cut into strips

8 oz/225 g new potatoes, halved

1 carrot, diced

2 celery stalks, sliced

2 leeks, sliced

3½ cups beef stock

8 baby corn, sliced

1 bouquet garni

2 tbsp dry sherry

salt and pepper

chopped fresh parsley, to garnish

crusty bread, to serve

COOK'S TIP

Make double the quantity of
soup and freeze the remainder in
a rigid container for later use.
When ready to use, leave in the
refrigerator to thaw thoroughly,
then heat until piping hot.

1 Heat the vegetable oil in a large pan. Add the strips of steak and cook for 3 minutes, turning constantly.

2 Add the potatoes, carrot, celery, and leeks. Cook, stirring constantly, for an additional 5 minutes.

3 Pour in the stock and bring to a boil over medium heat. Reduce the heat until the liquid is simmering gently, then add the baby corn and the bouquet garni.

4 Cook the soup for an additional 20 minutes, or until the meat and all the vegetables are tender.

5 Remove the bouquet garni from the pan and discard. Stir the sherry into the soup and season to taste with salt and pepper. Pour the soup into warmed soup bowls and garnish with parsley. Serve at once with crusty bread.

veal & ham soup

serves four

4 tbsp butter

1 onion, diced

1 carrot, diced

1 celery stalk, diced

1 lb/450 g veal, very thinly sliced

1 lb/450 g ham, thinly sliced

generous ⅓ cup all-purpose flour

4 cups beef stock

1 bay leaf

8 black peppercorns

pinch of salt

3 tbsp red currant jelly

⅔ cup cream sherry

3½ oz/100 g dried vermicelli

garlic croutons (see Cook's Tip),
     to garnish

COOK'S TIP

To make garlic croutons, cut
3 slices of day-old crustless white
bread into small cubes. Stir-fry
1–2 chopped garlic cloves
in 3 tablespoons of oil for
1–2 minutes. Remove the garlic
and cook the bread, stirring, until
golden. Remove and drain.

1 Melt the butter in a large pan.
Add the onion, carrot, celery,
veal, and ham and cook over low heat
for 6 minutes.

2 Sprinkle over the flour and cook,
stirring constantly, for an
additional 2 minutes. Gradually stir
in the stock, then add the bay leaf,
peppercorns, and salt. Bring to a boil
and let simmer for 1 hour.

3 Remove the pan from the heat
and add the red currant jelly and
sherry, stirring to combine. Set aside
for about 4 hours.

4 Discard the bay leaf. Reheat the
soup over very low heat until
warmed through. Meanwhile, cook
the vermicelli in a pan of lightly salted
boiling water for 10–12 minutes,
or until just tender. Stir into the soup
and transfer to serving bowls. Garnish
with garlic croutons.

tuscan veal broth

serves four

generous ¼ cup dried peas, soaked
for 2 hours and drained

2 lb/900 g boned neck of veal,
diced

5 cups beef stock

2½ cups water

generous ¼ cup pearl barley, rinsed

salt and pepper

1 large carrot, diced

1 small turnip (about 6 oz/175 g),
diced

1 large leek, thinly sliced

1 red onion, finely chopped

3½ oz/100 g tomatoes, chopped

1 fresh basil sprig

3½ oz/100 g dried vermicelli

1 Put the peas, veal, stock, and
water into a large pan and bring
to a boil over low heat. Using a slotted
spoon, skim off any scum that rises to
the surface of the liquid.

2 When all of the scum has been
removed, add the pearl barley
and a pinch of salt to the mixture.
Let simmer gently over low heat for
25 minutes.

3 Add the carrot, turnip, leek,
onion, tomatoes, and basil to the
pan and season to taste with salt and
pepper. Let simmer for about 2 hours,
skimming the surface, using a slotted
spoon, from time to time. Remove the
pan from the heat and set aside for
2 hours.

4 Set the pan over medium heat
and bring to a boil. Add the
vermicelli and cook for 12 minutes,
or until just tender. Taste and adjust the
seasoning, and remove and discard the
basil. Ladle into warmed soup bowls
and serve at once.

chinese potato & pork broth

serves four

4 cups chicken stock

2 large potatoes, diced

2 tbsp rice wine vinegar

2 tbsp cornstarch

4 tbsp water

4½ oz/125 g pork fillet, sliced

1 tbsp light soy sauce

1 tsp sesame oil

1 carrot, cut into very thin strips

1 tsp chopped fresh gingerroot

3 scallions, thinly sliced

1 red bell pepper, seeded and sliced

8 oz/225 g canned bamboo
shoots, drained

COOK'S TIP

For extra heat, add 1 chopped
fresh red chili or 1 teaspoon
of chili powder to the
soup in Step 5.

1 Place the stock, potatoes, and 1 tablespoon of the vinegar in a pan and bring to a boil. Reduce the heat until the stock is just simmering.

2 Mix the cornstarch with the water, then stir into the hot stock.

3 Return the stock to the boil, stirring until thickened, then reduce the heat until it is just simmering again.

4 Place the pork slices in a dish and season with the remaining vinegar, the soy sauce, and the oil.

5 Add the pork slices, carrot strips, and ginger to the stock and cook for 10 minutes. Stir in the scallions, bell pepper, and bamboo shoots. Cook for an additional 5 minutes. Pour the soup into warmed bowls and serve at once.

pork chili soup

serves three

2 tsp olive oil

1 lb 2 oz/500 g fresh lean
   ground pork

salt and pepper

1 onion, finely chopped

1 celery stalk, finely chopped

1 bell pepper, seeded and
   finely chopped

2–3 garlic cloves, finely chopped

14 oz/400 g canned chopped
   tomatoes in juice

3 tbsp tomato paste

2 cups chicken or meat stock

⅛ tsp ground coriander

⅛ tsp ground cumin

¼ tsp dried oregano

1 tsp mild chili powder, or to taste

chopped fresh cilantro leaves or
   parsley, to garnish

sour cream, to serve

COOK'S TIP

For a festive presentation, offer
additional accompaniments, such
as grated cheese, chopped
scallion, and guacamole.

---

1 Heat the oil in a large pan over medium–high heat. Add the pork and season to taste with salt and pepper, then cook until no longer pink, stirring frequently. Reduce the heat to medium and add the onion, celery, bell pepper, and garlic. Cover and cook for 5 minutes, stirring occasionally, until the onion is softened.

2 Add the tomatoes, tomato paste, and the stock, then add the coriander, cumin, oregano, and chili powder. Stir the ingredients in, to combine well.

3 Bring just to a boil, then reduce the heat to low and let simmer, covered, for 30–40 minutes, or until all the vegetables are very tender. Taste and adjust the seasoning, adding more chili powder if you like it hotter.

4 Ladle the chili into warmed bowls and sprinkle with cilantro. Hand the sour cream round separately, or top each serving with a spoonful.

spicy lamb soup with chickpeas

serves four–five

1–2 tbsp olive oil

1 lb/450 g lean boneless lamb, such as shoulder or neck fillet, trimmed of fat and cut into ½-inch/1-cm cubes

1 onion, finely chopped

2–3 garlic cloves, crushed

5 cups water

14 oz/400 g canned chopped tomatoes in juice

1 bay leaf

½ tsp dried thyme

½ tsp dried oregano

⅛ tsp ground cinnamon

¼ tsp ground cumin

¼ tsp ground turmeric

1 tsp harissa, or to taste

14 oz/400 g canned chickpeas, rinsed and drained

1 carrot, diced

1 potato, diced

1 zucchini, cut into fourths lengthwise and sliced

scant 1 cup fresh shelled or thawed frozen peas

chopped fresh mint or cilantro leaves, to garnish

1 Heat the oil in a large pan or cast-iron casserole over medium–high heat. Add the lamb, in batches if necessary to avoid crowding the pan, and cook until evenly browned on all sides, adding a little more oil if needed. Remove the meat with a slotted spoon when browned.

2 Reduce the heat and add the onion and garlic. Cook, stirring frequently, for 1–2 minutes.

3 Add the water and return all the meat to the pan. Bring just to a boil and skim off any scum that rises to the surface. Reduce the heat and stir in the tomatoes, bay leaf, thyme, oregano, cinnamon, cumin, turmeric, and harissa. Let simmer for 1 hour, or until the meat is very tender. Remove and discard the bay leaf.

4 Stir in the chickpeas, carrot, and potato and let simmer for 15 minutes. Add the zucchini and peas and continue simmering for 15–20 minutes, or until all the vegetables are tender.

5 Adjust the seasoning, adding more harissa, if wished. Ladle the soup into warmed bowls and garnish with mint.

rich beef stew

serves four

1 tbsp oil

1 tbsp butter

8 oz/225 g pearl onions, peeled
    and halved

1 lb 5 oz/600 g stewing steak, diced
    into 1½-inch/4-cm chunks

1¼ cups beef stock

⅔ cup red wine

4 tbsp chopped fresh oregano

1 tbsp sugar

1 orange

¼ cup dried porcini or other
    dried mushrooms

4 tbsp warm water

8 oz/225 g fresh plum tomatoes

cooked rice or potatoes, to serve

VARIATION

Instead of fresh tomatoes, try
using sun-dried tomatoes, cut
into wide strips, if you prefer.

1 Preheat the oven to 350°F/180°C. Heat the oil and butter in a skillet. Add the onions and cook for 5 minutes, or until golden. Remove with a slotted spoon, set aside, and keep warm.

2 Add the beef to the skillet and cook, stirring, for 5 minutes, or until browned all over.

3 Return the onions to the skillet and add the stock, wine, oregano, and sugar, stirring to mix well. Transfer the mixture to an ovenproof casserole.

4 Pare the rind from the orange and cut it into strips. Slice the orange flesh into rings. Add the orange rings and the rind to the casserole. Cook in the oven for 1¼ hours.

5 Soak the mushrooms for 30 minutes in a small bowl containing the warm water.

6 Peel and halve the tomatoes. Add the tomatoes, mushrooms, and their soaking liquid to the casserole. Cook for an additional 20 minutes, or until the beef is tender and the juices have thickened. Serve with cooked rice or potatoes.

beef & orange curry

serves four

1 tbsp vegetable oil

8 oz/225 g shallots, halved

2 garlic cloves, crushed

1 lb/450 g lean round steak or
   short loin beef, trimmed and
   cut into ¾-inch/2-cm cubes

3 tbsp curry paste

2 cups beef stock

4 oranges

2 tsp cornstarch

salt and pepper

2 tbsp chopped cilantro, to garnish

boiled basmati rice, to serve

RAITA

½ cucumber, finely diced

3 tbsp chopped fresh mint

⅔ cup lowfat plain yogurt

1 Heat the oil in a large pan. Add the shallots, garlic, and beef cubes and cook over low heat, stirring occasionally, for 5 minutes, or until the beef is evenly browned all over.

2 Blend together the curry paste and stock. Add the mixture to the beef and stir to mix thoroughly. Bring to a boil, cover, and simmer for about 1 hour.

3 Grate the rind of 1 orange. Squeeze the juice from the orange and from 1 other. Peel the other 2 oranges, removing the pith. Slice between each segment and remove the flesh.

4 Blend the cornstarch with the orange juice. At the end of the cooking time, stir the orange rind into the beef with the orange and cornstarch mixture. Bring to a boil and simmer, stirring constantly, for 3–4 minutes, or until the sauce thickens. Season to taste with salt and pepper and stir in the orange segments.

5 To make the Raita, mix the cucumber with the mint and stir in the yogurt. Season to taste with salt and pepper.

6 Serve the curry with rice and the cucumber Raita, garnished with the chopped cilantro.

beef & tomato gratin

serves four

1½ cups fresh lean ground beef

1 large onion, finely chopped

1 tsp dried mixed herbs

1 tbsp all-purpose flour

1¼ cups beef stock

1 tbsp tomato paste

salt and pepper

2 large tomatoes, thinly sliced

4 zucchini, thinly sliced

2 tbsp cornstarch

1¼ cups skim milk

⅔ cup ricotta

1 egg yolk

4 tbsp freshly grated
   Parmesan cheese

TO SERVE

crusty bread

steamed vegetables

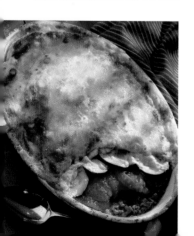

1 Preheat the oven to 375°F/190°C. In a large skillet, dry-fry the beef and onion for 4–5 minutes, or until browned.

2 Stir in the herbs, flour, stock, and tomato paste, and season to taste with salt and pepper. Bring to a boil, then reduce the heat and let simmer for 30 minutes, or until thickened.

3 Transfer the beef mixture to an ovenproof gratin dish. Cover with a layer of the sliced tomatoes and then add a layer of sliced zucchini. Set aside until required.

4 Blend the cornstarch with a little of the milk in a small bowl. Pour the remaining milk into a pan and bring to a boil. Add the cornstarch mixture and then cook, stirring, for 1–2 minutes, or until thickened. Remove from the heat and beat in the ricotta and egg yolk. Season well.

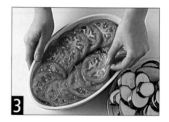

5 Spread the white sauce over the layer of zucchini. Place the dish on a baking sheet and sprinkle with Parmesan cheese. Bake in the oven for 25–30 minutes, or until golden brown. Serve with crusty bread and steamed vegetables.

michoacan beef

serves four–six

about 3 tbsp all-purpose flour

salt and pepper

2 lb 4 oz/1 kg stewing beef, cut into
large bite-size pieces

2 tbsp vegetable oil

2 onions, chopped

5 garlic cloves, chopped

14 oz/400 g tomatoes, diced

1½ dried chipotle chilies,
reconstituted (see Cook's Tip,
page 78), seeded and cut into
thin strips, or a few shakes of
bottled chipotle salsa

6 cups beef stock

12 oz/350 g green beans

pinch of sugar

TO SERVE

cooked kidney beans

freshly cooked rice

COOK'S TIP

This is traditionally made with *nopales*—edible cacti—which gives the dish a distinctive flavor. Look out for them in specialty stores. For this recipe you need 12–14 oz/350–400 g canned nopales, or fresh nopales, peeled, sliced, and blanched. Add them to the stew with the tomatoes.

1 Place the flour in a large bowl and season to taste with salt and pepper. Add the beef and toss to coat well. Remove the beef from the bowl, shaking off the excess flour.

2 Heat the oil in a skillet. Add the beef and brown briefly over high heat. Reduce the heat to medium and add the onions and garlic, then cook for 2 minutes.

3 Add the tomatoes, chilies, and stock, then cover and let simmer over low heat for 1½ hours, or until the meat is very tender, adding the green beans and sugar 15 minutes before the end of the cooking time. Skim off any fat that rises to the surface from time to time.

4 Transfer to individual warmed bowls and serve with kidney beans and rice.

beef cooked in whole spices

serves four

1¼ cups oil

3 onions, finely chopped

1-inch/2.5-cm piece fresh
   gingerroot, grated

4 garlic cloves, sliced

2 cinnamon sticks

3 green cardamoms

3 cloves

4 black peppercorns

6 dried red chilies

⅔ cup plain yogurt

1 lb/450 g lean beef, cubed

3 fresh green chilies, chopped

2½ cups water

VARIATION

Substitute lamb for the beef in
this recipe, if you prefer.

---

1 Heat the oil in a skillet. Add the onions and sauté, stirring, until golden brown.

2 Reduce the heat, then add the ginger, garlic, cinnamon sticks, cardamoms, cloves, peppercorns, and dried chilies to the skillet and stir-fry for 5 minutes. In a bowl, whisk the yogurt with a fork. Add the yogurt to the onion mixture in the skillet and stir to combine.

3 Add the beef and 2 of the fresh chilies to the skillet and stir-fry the mixture for 5–7 minutes.

4 Gradually add the water to the skillet, stirring well. Cover and cook the beef and spice mixture for 1 hour, stirring and adding more water if necessary.

5 When thoroughly cooked through, remove the skillet from the heat and transfer the beef and spice mixture to a warmed serving dish. Garnish with the remaining chopped fresh chili.

citrus osso bucco

serves six

1–2 tbsp all-purpose flour

salt and pepper

6 meaty slices veal

2 lb 4 oz/1 kg fresh tomatoes,
    peeled, seeded, and diced, or
    1 lb 12 oz/800 g canned
    chopped tomatoes

1–2 tbsp olive oil

9 oz/250 g onions, very
    finely chopped

9 oz/250 g carrots, finely diced

1 cup dry white wine

1 cup veal stock

6 large fresh basil leaves, torn

1 large garlic clove, very
    finely chopped

finely grated rind of 1 large lemon

finely grated rind of 1 orange

2 tbsp finely chopped fresh
    flatleaf parsley

1 Put the flour in a plastic bag and season to taste with salt and pepper. Add the veal, a few pieces at a time, and shake until well coated. Remove and shake off the excess flour.

2 If using canned tomatoes, put them in a nylon strainer and let drain.

3 Heat 1 tablespoon of the oil in a large, flameproof casserole. Add the veal and cook for 10 minutes on each side until well browned. Remove from the casserole.

4 Add 1–2 teaspoons more oil to the casserole if necessary. Add the onions and cook, stirring, for 5 minutes, or until soft. Stir in the carrots and cook until softened.

5 Add the tomatoes, wine, stock, and basil and return the osso bucco to the casserole. Bring to a boil, then reduce the heat and let simmer, covered, for 1 hour. Check that the meat is tender with the tip of a knife. If not, continue cooking for 10 minutes and test again.

6 When the meat is tender, sprinkle with the garlic and lemon and orange rinds. Cover and cook over low heat for an additional 10 minutes.

7 Taste and adjust the seasoning if necessary. Sprinkle with the parsley and serve at once.

chili con carne

serves four

1 lb 10 oz/750 g lean rump or
  stewing steak

2 tbsp vegetable oil

1 large onion, sliced

2–4 garlic cloves, crushed

1 tbsp all-purpose flour

scant 2 cups tomato juice

14 oz/400 g canned tomatoes

1–2 tbsp sweet chili sauce

1 tsp ground cumin

salt and pepper

15 oz/425 g canned red kidney
  beans, drained

½ teaspoon dried oregano

1–2 tbsp chopped fresh parsley

chopped fresh herbs, to garnish

boiled rice and tortillas, to serve

2 Add the onion and garlic to the casserole and cook until lightly browned. Stir in the flour and cook for 1–2 minutes. Stir in the tomato juice and tomatoes and bring to a boil. Return the beef to the casserole and add the chili sauce, cumin, and salt and pepper to taste. Cover and cook in the oven for 1½ hours, or until almost tender.

3 Stir in the beans, oregano, and parsley and adjust the seasoning to taste. Cover the casserole and return to the oven for 45 minutes. Sprinkle with herbs and serve with boiled rice and tortillas.

COOK'S TIP

Because chili con carne requires quite a lengthy cooking time, it is worth preparing double the quantity you need and freezing half of it to serve another time.

1 Preheat the oven to 325°F/160°C. Cut the beef into ¾-inch/2-cm cubes. Heat the oil in an ovenproof casserole. Cook the beef until browned. Remove from the casserole.

cornmeal with rabbit stew

serves four

butter, for greasing

scant 2 cups cornmeal

1 tbsp coarse sea salt

5 cups water

4 tbsp olive oil

4 lb 8 oz/2 kg rabbit joints

3 garlic cloves, peeled

3 shallots, sliced

⅔ cup red wine

1 carrot, sliced

1 celery stalk, sliced

2 bay leaves

1 fresh rosemary sprig

3 tomatoes, peeled and diced

½ cup pitted black olives

1¼ cups water

salt and pepper

2 Meanwhile, heat the oil in a large pan and add the rabbit pieces, garlic, and shallots. Cook for 10 minutes, or until browned.

3 Stir in the wine and cook for an additional 5 minutes.

4 Add the carrot, celery, bay leaves, rosemary, tomatoes, olives, and water. Cover the pan and let simmer for 45 minutes, or until the rabbit is tender. Season to taste with salt and pepper. To serve, spoon or cut a portion of cornmeal and place on each serving plate. Top with a ladleful of rabbit stew. Serve at once.

1 Preheat the oven to 375°F/190°C. Grease a large, ovenproof dish with a little butter. Mix the cornmeal, salt, and water together in a large pan, whisking well to prevent lumps from forming. Bring to a boil and boil for 10 minutes, stirring vigorously and constantly. Turn the cornmeal into the prepared dish and bake in the oven for 40 minutes.

maltese rabbit with fennel

serves four

5 tbsp olive oil

2 large fennel bulbs, sliced

2 carrots, diced

1 large garlic clove, crushed

1 tbsp fennel seeds

about 4 tbsp all-purpose flour

salt and pepper

2 wild rabbits, jointed

1 cup dry white wine

1 cup water

1 bouquet garni of 2 fresh
   flatleaf parsley sprigs,
    1 fresh rosemary sprig, and
    1 bay leaf, tied in a 3-inch/
    7.5-cm piece of celery

thick, crusty bread, to serve

TO GARNISH

finely chopped fresh flatleaf
   parsley or cilantro

fresh rosemary sprigs

1 Heat 3 tablespoons of the oil in a large, ovenproof casserole over medium heat. Add the fennel and carrots and cook, stirring occasionally, for 5 minutes. Stir in the garlic and fennel seeds and cook for an additional 2 minutes, or until the fennel is tender. Remove the fennel and carrots from the casserole with a slotted spoon and set aside.

2 Put the flour in a plastic bag and season to taste with salt and pepper. Add 2 rabbit pieces and shake to lightly coat, then shake off any excess flour. Continue until all the pieces of rabbit are coated, adding more flour if necessary.

3 Add the remaining oil to the casserole. Sauté the rabbit pieces for 5 minutes on each side, or until golden brown, working in batches. Remove the rabbit from the casserole as it is cooked.

4 Pour in the wine and bring to a boil, stirring to scrape up all the sediment from the bottom. Return the rabbit pieces, fennel, and carrots to the casserole and pour in the water. Add the bouquet garni and season to taste with salt and pepper.

5 Bring to a boil, then reduce the heat and cover. Let simmer for 1¼ hours, or until the rabbit is tender.

6 Discard the bouquet garni. Garnish with herbs and serve straight from the casserole with lots of bread to mop up the juices.

country pork with onions

serves four

2 large pork hand or leg joints

2 large garlic cloves, sliced

3 tbsp olive oil

2 carrots, finely chopped

2 celery stalks, finely chopped

1 large onion, finely chopped

2 fresh thyme sprigs, broken
    into pieces

2 fresh rosemary sprigs, broken
    into pieces

1 large bay leaf

1 cup dry white wine

1 cup water

pepper

20 pearl onions

coarsely chopped fresh flatleaf
    parsley, to garnish

1 Preheat the oven to 325°F/160°C. Using the tip of a sharp knife, make slits all over the pork and insert the garlic slices.

2 Heat 1 tablespoon of the oil in an ovenproof casserole over medium heat. Add the carrots, celery, and onion. Cook, stirring occasionally, for 10 minutes, or until softened.

3 Place the pork on top of the vegetables. Sprinkle the thyme and rosemary over the meat. Add the bay leaf, wine, and water and season to taste with pepper.

4 Bring to a boil, then remove from the heat. Cover tightly and cook in the oven for 3½ hours, or until the meat is very tender.

5 Meanwhile, put the onions in a heatproof bowl, then pour over boiling water to cover and set aside for 1 minute. Drain, then slip off all the skins. Heat the remaining oil in a large, heavy-bottom skillet. Add the onions and partially cover, then cook over low heat for 15 minutes, shaking the skillet occasionally, until the onions are just starting to turn golden.

6 When the pork is tender, add the onions to the casserole. Return to the oven for an additional 15 minutes. Remove the pork and onions from the casserole and keep warm.

7 Using a large, metal spoon, skim off as much fat as possible from the surface of the cooking liquid. Strain the cooking liquid into a bowl, pressing down lightly to extract the flavor; reserve the strained vegetables. Adjust the seasoning.

8 Cut the pork from the bones, if wished, then arrange on a serving platter with the onions and strained vegetables. Spoon the sauce over the meat and vegetables. Garnish with parsley.

sliced beef with yogurt

serves four

1 lb/450 g lean beef slices, cut into
  1-inch/2.5-cm slices
5 tbsp plain yogurt
1 tsp finely chopped fresh
  gingerroot
1 tsp crushed garlic
1 tsp chili powder
pinch of ground turmeric
2 tsp garam masala
1 tsp salt
2 green cardamoms
1 tsp black cumin seeds
generous ½ cup ground almonds
1 tbsp dry unsweetened coconut
1 tbsp poppy seeds
1 tbsp sesame seeds
1¼ cups vegetable oil
2 onions, finely chopped
1¼ cups water
2 fresh green chilies
few cilantro leaves, chopped

1 Place the beef in a large bowl. Combine with the yogurt, ginger, garlic, chili powder, turmeric, garam masala, salt, cardamoms, and cumin seeds and set aside until required.

2 Dry-fry the almonds, coconut, and poppy and sesame seeds in a heavy-bottom skillet until golden, shaking the skillet occasionally.

3 Transfer the spice mixture to a food processor and process until finely ground. (Add 1 tablespoon of water to blend, if necessary.) Add the ground spice mixture to the meat mixture and combine.

4 Heat a little of the oil in a large skillet, then add the onions and cook until golden brown. Remove the onions from the skillet. Heat the remaining oil and stir-fry the beef mixture for 5 minutes, then return the onions to the skillet and stir-fry for an additional 5–7 minutes. Add the water and cover, then let simmer over low heat, stirring occasionally, for 25–30 minutes. Add the chilies and cilantro and serve hot.

potato, beef & peanut pot

serves four

- 1 tbsp vegetable oil
- 5 tbsp butter
- 1 lb/450 g lean steak, cut into thin strips
- 1 onion, halved and sliced
- 2 garlic cloves, crushed
- 1 lb 5 oz/600 g waxy potatoes, cubed
- ½ tsp paprika
- 4 tbsp crunchy peanut butter
- 2½ cups beef stock
- 4 tbsp unsalted peanuts
- 2 tsp light soy sauce
- 2 oz/55 g sugar snap peas
- 1 red bell pepper, seeded and cut into strips
- few sprigs of fresh parsley, to garnish (optional)

1 Heat the oil and butter in an ovenproof casserole.

2 Add the steak strips and cook them gently, stirring and turning the meat, for 3–4 minutes, or until sealed on all sides.

3 Add the onion and garlic to the meat and cook for an additional 2 minutes, stirring constantly.

4 Add the potato cubes and cook for 3–4 minutes, or until starting to brown.

5 Stir in the paprika and peanut butter, then gradually stir in the stock. Bring the mixture to a boil, stirring frequently.

6 Add the peanuts, soy sauce, sugar snap peas, and bell pepper.

7 Cover the casserole and cook over low heat for 45 minutes, or until the beef is cooked right through. Garnish the dish with parsley sprigs, if wished, and serve at once.

pork stroganoff

12 oz/350 g lean pork fillet

1 tbsp vegetable oil

1 onion, chopped

2 garlic cloves, crushed

2 tbsp all-purpose flour

2 tbsp tomato paste

scant 2 cups chicken or
   vegetable stock

4½ oz/125 g white
   mushrooms, sliced

1 large green bell pepper, seeded
   and diced

salt and pepper

½ tsp ground nutmeg, plus extra
   to garnish

4 tbsp lowfat plain yogurt, plus
   extra to serve

freshly boiled white rice, to serve

1 Trim away any excess fat
  and membrane from the pork,
then cut the meat into slices ½ inch/
1 cm thick.

2 Heat the oil in a large pan over
  medium heat, then add the pork,
onion, and garlic and cook for
4–5 minutes, or until lightly browned.

3 Stir in the flour and tomato paste,
  then pour in the stock and stir to
mix thoroughly.

COOK'S TIP

You can buy ready-made stock
from leading stores. Although
more expensive, it is more
nutritious than using bouillon
cubes, which can be high in salt
and artificial flavorings.

4 Add the mushrooms, green bell
  pepper, salt and pepper to taste,
and nutmeg. Bring to a boil, then cover
and let simmer for 20 minutes, or until
the pork is cooked through.

5 Remove the pan from the heat
  and let cool slightly, then stir in
the yogurt. Serve the pork and sauce
on a bed of rice, topped with an extra
spoonful of yogurt and garnished with
a dusting of nutmeg.

italian sausage & bean casserole

serves four

1 green bell pepper

8 Italian sausages

1 tbsp olive oil

1 large onion, chopped

2 garlic cloves, chopped

8 oz/225 g fresh tomatoes, peeled
and chopped, or 14 oz/400 g
canned tomatoes, chopped

2 tbsp sun-dried tomato paste

14 oz/400 g canned cannellini
beans, drained

mashed potatoes or rice, to serve

COOK'S TIP

Italian sausages are coarse in
texture and have quite a
strong flavor. They can be
found in specialty sausage
stores, Italian delicatessens,
and some larger supermarkets.
Game sausages can be used
instead in this recipe.

1 Preheat the broiler. Seed the bell
pepper and cut it into thin strips.

2 Prick the Italian sausages all
over with a fork. Cook under the
hot broiler, turning occasionally, for
10–12 minutes, or until browned. Cut
into chunks, set aside, and keep warm.

3 Heat the oil in a large skillet.
Add the onion, garlic, and bell
pepper and cook, stirring occasionally,
for 4 minutes, or until softened.

4 Add the tomatoes to the skillet
and let the mixture simmer,
stirring occasionally, for 5 minutes,
or until slightly reduced and thickened.

5 Stir the sun-dried tomato paste,
beans, and sausages into the
mixture and cook for 4–5 minutes, or
until piping hot. Add 4–5 tablespoons
of water if the mixture becomes too dry
during cooking.

6 Transfer the casserole to warmed
serving plates and serve with
mashed potatoes or cooked rice.

tomatoes cooked with meat & yogurt

serves two–four

- 1 tsp garam masala
- 1 tsp finely chopped fresh gingerroot
- 1 garlic clove, crushed
- 2 black cardamoms
- 1 tsp chili powder
- ½ tsp black cumin seeds
- 2 x 1-inch/2.5-cm cinnamon sticks
- 1 tsp salt
- ⅔ cup plain yogurt
- 1 lb 2 oz/500 g lean lamb, cubed
- ⅔ cup oil
- 2 onions, sliced
- 2½ cups water
- 2 large, firm tomatoes,
  cut into fourths
- 2 tbsp lemon juice
- 2 fresh green chilies, chopped,
  to garnish

1 In a large mixing bowl, mix together the garam masala, ginger, garlic, cardamoms, chili powder, cumin seeds, cinnamon sticks, salt, and the yogurt until well combined.

2 Add the lamb to the yogurt and spice mixture and mix well to coat the meat. Set aside. Heat the oil in a large skillet, then add the onions and cook until golden brown.

3 Add the lamb to the skillet and stir-fry for 5 minutes. Reduce the heat and add the water, then cover the skillet and let simmer for 1 hour, stirring occasionally.

4 Add the tomatoes to the curry and sprinkle with the lemon juice. Let the curry simmer for an additional 7–10 minutes.

5 Garnish the curry with the green chilies, and serve hot.

beef korma with almonds

serves four

1¼ cups vegetable oil

3 onions, finely chopped

2 lb 4 oz/1 kg lean beef, cubed

1½ tsp garam masala

1½ tsp ground coriander

1½ tsp finely chopped fresh
   gingerroot

1½ tsp crushed garlic

1 tsp salt

⅔ cup plain yogurt

2 cloves

3 green cardamoms

4 black peppercorns

2½ cups water

chapatis, to serve

TO GARNISH

6 whole almonds, soaked, peeled,
   and chopped

2 fresh green chilies, chopped

few cilantro leaves

1 Heat the oil in a skillet, then add the onions and stir-fry until golden brown. Remove half the onions from the skillet and set aside.

2 Add the meat to the remaining onions in the skillet and stir-fry for 5 minutes. Remove the skillet from the heat.

3 Combine the garam masala, ground coriander, ginger, garlic, salt, and yogurt in a large bowl. Gradually add the meat to the spice mixture and mix to coat well. Return the meat mixture to the skillet. Cook, stirring constantly, for 5–7 minutes, or until the mixture is golden.

4 Add the cloves, cardamoms, and peppercorns, then add the water, and reduce the heat. Cover and let simmer for 45–60 minutes. If necessary, add another 1¼ cups water and cook for an additional 10–15 minutes, stirring occasionally.

5 Just before serving, garnish with the reserved onions, almonds, chilies, and the cilantro leaves. Serve with chapatis.

traditional provençal daube

serves four–six

1 lb 9 oz/700 g boneless lean
   stewing beef, such as leg, cut
   into 2-inch/5-cm pieces

1¾ cups full-bodied dry
   red wine

2 tbsp olive oil

4 large garlic cloves, crushed

4 shallots, thinly sliced

9 oz/250 g unsmoked lardons

5–6 tbsp all-purpose flour

salt and pepper

9 oz/250 g large cremini
   mushrooms, sliced

14 oz/400 g canned
   chopped tomatoes

1 large bouquet garni of 1 bay leaf,
   2 dried thyme sprigs, and
   2 fresh parsley sprigs, tied in a
   3-inch/7.5-cm piece of celery

2-inch/5-cm strip of dried
   orange rind

2 cups beef stock

1¾ oz/50 g canned anchovies in oil

2 tbsp capers in brine, rinsed
   and drained

2 tbsp red wine vinegar

2 tbsp finely chopped fresh parsley

1 Place the beef, wine, oil, half the garlic, and shallots in a non-metallic bowl. Cover and let chill for at least 4 hours, stirring occasionally.

2 Meanwhile, place the lardons in a pan of water and bring to a boil. Let simmer for 10 minutes. Drain.

3 Place 4 tablespoons of the flour in a bowl and stir in 2 tablespoons water to make a thick paste. Cover with plastic wrap and set aside.

4 Preheat the oven to 325°F/160°C. Strain the beef, reserving the marinade. Pat dry and toss in the remaining flour, seasoned.

5 Arrange a layer of lardons, mushrooms, and tomatoes, then beef in a large, ovenproof casserole. Layer the remaining ingredients and tuck in the bouquet garni and rind.

6 Pour in the stock and reserved marinade. Spread the flour paste around the rim of the casserole. Press on the lid to make a tight seal (make more paste if necessary).

7 Cook in the oven for 2½ hours. Meanwhile, drain the anchovies, then mash with the capers and remaining garlic in a mortar with a pestle.

8 Remove the casserole from the oven and break the seal, then stir in the mashed anchovies, vinegar, and parsley. Cover and cook for an additional 1–1½ hours, or until the meat is tender. Taste and adjust the seasoning and serve at once.

hot spicy lamb in sauce

serves six–eight

¾ cup oil

2 lb 4 oz/1 kg lean leg of lamb,
    cut into large pieces

1 tbsp garam masala

5 onions, chopped

⅔ cup plain yogurt

2 tbsp tomato paste

2 tsp finely chopped fresh
    gingerroot

2 garlic cloves, crushed

1½ tsp salt

2 tsp chili powder

1 tbsp ground coriander

2 tsp ground nutmeg

3½ cups water

1 tbsp ground fennel seeds

1 tbsp paprika

1 tbsp besan (gram flour)

3 bay leaves

1 tbsp all-purpose flour

2 tbsp warm water

2–3 fresh green chilies, chopped

2 tbsp chopped cilantro, plus extra
    to garnish

thin slivers of fresh gingerroot,
    to garnish

naan bread, to serve

1 Heat the oil in a skillet and add the meat and half the garam masala. Stir-fry the mixture for 7–10 minutes, or until the meat is well coated. Using a slotted spoon, remove the meat and set aside.

2 Add the onions to the skillet and cook until golden brown. Return the meat to the skillet, reduce the heat and let simmer, stirring occasionally.

3 In a bowl, mix together the yogurt, tomato paste, ginger, garlic, salt, chili powder, ground coriander, nutmeg, and the remaining garam masala. Pour the mixture over the meat and stir-fry, mixing the spices well into the meat, for 5–7 minutes.

4 Stir in half the water, then add the fennel seeds, paprika, and besan. Add the remaining water and the bay leaves, then reduce the heat and cook, covered, for 1 hour, stirring occasionally.

5 Mix the flour with the warm water and pour the mixture over the curry. Sprinkle with the chilies and the cilantro and cook until the meat is tender and the sauce thickens. Garnish with cilantro and ginger and serve with naan bread.

spicy pork with prunes

serves four–six

1 pork joint, such as leg or shoulder,
  weighing 3 lb 5 oz/1.5 kg

juice of 2–3 limes

10 garlic cloves, chopped

3–4 tbsp mild chili powder

4 tbsp vegetable oil

salt

2 onions, chopped

scant 2½ cups chicken stock

25 small tart tomatoes, coarsely
  chopped

25 prunes, pitted

1–2 tsp sugar

pinch of ground cinnamon

pinch of ground allspice

pinch of ground cumin

warmed corn tortillas, to serve

1 In a nonmetallic dish, combine
  the pork with the lime juice,
garlic, chili powder, half the oil, and
salt to taste. Cover and let marinate
in the refrigerator overnight.

2 Preheat the oven to 350°F/180°C.
  Remove the pork from the
marinade. Wipe the pork dry with
paper towels and reserve the
marinade. Heat the remaining oil in
an ovenproof casserole and brown the
pork evenly until just golden. Add the
onions, the reserved marinade, and
stock. Cover and cook in the oven for
2–3 hours, or until the pork is tender.

3 Remove from the oven. Spoon
  off the fat from the surface of the
cooking liquid and add the tomatoes.
Cook for an additional 20 minutes, or
until the tomatoes are tender. Mash the
tomatoes into a coarse purée. Add the
prunes and sugar, then adjust the
seasoning, adding cinnamon, allspice,
and cumin to taste, as well as extra
chili powder, if wished.

4 Increase the oven temperature to
  400°F/200°C and return the meat
and sauce to the oven for an additional
20–30 minutes, or until the meat
has browned on top and the juices
have thickened.

5 Remove the meat from the
  casserole and set aside for a few
minutes. Carefully carve it into thin
slices and spoon the sauce over the
top. Serve with warmed corn tortillas.

basque pork & beans

serves four–six

generous 1 cup dried cannellini
beans, soaked in water overnight

olive oil, for cooking

1 lb 5 oz/600 g boneless leg of
pork, cut into 2-inch/5-cm chunks

1 large onion, sliced

3 large garlic cloves, crushed

14 oz/400 g canned
chopped tomatoes

2 green bell peppers, seeded
and sliced

finely grated rind of 1 large orange

salt and pepper

finely chopped fresh parsley,
to garnish

1 Preheat the oven to 350°F/180°C.
Drain the beans and put in a
large pan with fresh water to cover.
Bring to a boil and boil rapidly for
10 minutes. Reduce the heat and let
simmer for 20 minutes. Drain.

2 Add enough oil to cover the
bottom of a skillet in a very thin
layer. Heat the oil over medium heat,
then add a few pieces of the pork and
cook on all sides until brown. Remove
from the skillet and set aside. Repeat
with the remaining pork.

3 Add 1 tablespoon of oil to the
skillet, if necessary, then add the
onion and cook for 3 minutes. Stir in
the garlic and cook for 2 minutes.
Return the pork to the skillet.

4 Add the tomatoes and bring to a
boil. Reduce the heat and stir in
the bell pepper slices, orange rind, and
the drained beans. Season to taste
with salt and pepper.

5 Transfer to a casserole. Cover the
casserole and cook in the oven for
45 minutes, or until the beans and
pork are tender. Sprinkle with chopped
parsley and serve at once straight from
the casserole.

savory hotchpotch

serves four

8 middle neck lean lamb chops,
  neck of lamb, or any lean
  stewing lamb

salt and pepper

1–2 garlic cloves, crushed

2 lamb's kidneys (optional)

1 large onion, thinly sliced

1 leek, sliced

2–3 carrots, sliced

1 tsp chopped fresh tarragon or
  sage, or ½ tsp dried tarragon
  or sage

2 lb 4 oz/1 kg potatoes, thinly sliced

1¼ cups stock

2 tbsp margarine, melted, or 1 tbsp
  vegetable oil

chopped fresh parsley, to garnish

1 Preheat the oven to 350°F/180°C. Trim any excess fat from the lamb, season well with salt and pepper, and arrange in a large, ovenproof casserole. Sprinkle with crushed garlic.

2 If using kidneys, remove the skin, then halve and cut out the cores. Chop into pieces and sprinkle over the lamb.

3 Place the vegetables over the lamb, letting the pieces slip in between the meat, then sprinkle with the herbs.

4 Arrange the potato slices on top of the meat and vegetables, in an overlapping pattern.

5 Bring the stock to a boil and season to taste with salt and pepper, then pour over the casserole.

6 Brush the potatoes with the melted margarine, then cover with greased foil or a lid, and cook in the oven for 1½ hours.

7 Remove the foil or lid from the casserole, then increase the temperature to 425°F/220°C and return the casserole to the oven for 30 minutes, or until the potatoes are browned.

8 Garnish the hotchpotch with parsley and serve at once.

lamb with onions & dried mango powder

serves four

4 onions

1¼ cups oil

1 tsp finely chopped fresh
gingerroot

1 garlic clove, crushed

1 tsp chili powder

pinch of ground turmeric

1 tsp salt

3 fresh green chilies, chopped

1 lb/450 g lean lamb, cubed

2½ cups water

1½ tsp aamchoor (dried
mango powder)

1 small bunch cilantro, chopped

boiled rice, to serve

1 Using a sharp knife, finely chop 3 of the onions.

2 Heat half the oil in a skillet, then add the onions and sauté until golden brown. Reduce the heat and add the ginger, garlic, chili powder, turmeric, and salt. Stir-fry the mixture for 5 minutes, then add 2 of the chopped chilies.

3 Add the lamb to the skillet and stir-fry the mixture for an additional 7 minutes.

COOK'S TIP
Aamchoor is made from dried mangoes. It has a sour taste and can be bought in jars.

4 Add the water to the skillet, then cover and cook over low heat, stirring occasionally, for 35–45 minutes, or until the lamb is tender.

5 Meanwhile, slice the remaining onion. Heat the remaining oil in a skillet and sauté the onion until golden. Set aside.

6 Once the lamb is tender, add the aamchoor, the remaining chili, and the chopped cilantro and stir-fry for 3–5 minutes.

7 Transfer the curry to a serving dish and pour the sautéed onion slices and oil down the center. Serve hot, with rice.

red pork curry

serves four–six

2 lb/900 g boneless pork
shoulder, sliced

3 cups coconut milk

2 fresh red chilies, seeded
and sliced

2 tbsp Thai fish sauce

2 tsp brown sugar

1 red bell pepper, seeded and sliced

6 kaffir lime leaves, shredded

½ bunch fresh mint
leaves, shredded

½ bunch fresh Thai basil leaves or
ordinary basil, shredded

Thai fragrant rice, to serve

RED CURRY PASTE

1 tbsp coriander seeds

2 tsp cumin seeds

2 tsp black or white peppercorns

1 tsp salt

5–8 dried hot red chilies

3–4 shallots, chopped

6–8 garlic cloves

2-inch/5-cm piece fresh gingerroot,
coarsely chopped

2 kaffir lime leaves

1 tbsp ground chili powder

1 tbsp shrimp paste

2 lemongrass stems, thinly sliced

1 To make the red curry paste, grind the coriander and cumin seeds, peppercorns, and salt to a fine powder in a mortar with a pestle. Add the dried chilies, 1 at a time according to taste, until ground.

2 Put the shallots, garlic, ginger, lime leaves, chili powder, and shrimp paste in a food processor. Process for 1 minute. Add the ground spices and process again. Adding water, a few drops at a time, continue to process until a thick paste forms. Scrape into a bowl and stir in the lemongrass.

3 Put about half the red curry paste in a large, deep, heavy-bottom skillet with the pork. Cook over medium heat, stirring gently, for 2–3 minutes, or until the pork is evenly coated and starts to brown.

4 Stir in the coconut milk and bring to a boil. Cook, stirring frequently, for 10 minutes. Reduce the heat, then stir in the fresh chilies, fish sauce, and sugar and let simmer for 20 minutes. Add the bell pepper and let simmer for an additional 10 minutes.

5 Chop the lime leaves and add to the curry with half the mint and basil. Transfer to a serving dish and sprinkle with the remaining mint and basil, then serve with the rice.

lamb biryani

serves six

⅔ cup milk

1 tsp saffron threads

5 tbsp pure or vegetable ghee

3 onions, sliced

2 lb 4 oz/1 kg lean lamb, cubed

7 tbsp plain yogurt

1½ tsp finely chopped fresh
 gingerroot

1–2 garlic cloves, crushed

2 tsp garam masala

2 tsp salt

¼ tsp ground turmeric

2½ cups water

1 lb/450 g basmati rice

2 tsp black cumin seeds

3 green cardamoms

4 tbsp lemon juice

2 fresh green chilies

¼ bunch cilantro, chopped

1 Boil the milk in a pan with the saffron and set aside. Heat the ghee in a large pan and sauté the onions until golden. Remove half the onions and ghee from the pan and set aside in a bowl.

2 Combine the meat, yogurt, ginger, garlic, garam masala, half the salt, and turmeric in a large bowl and mix well.

3 Return the pan with the ghee and onions to the heat. Add the meat mixture, stir for 3 minutes, then add the water. Cook over low heat for 45 minutes, stirring occasionally. Check to see whether the meat is tender; if not, add ⅔ cup water and cook for an additional 15 minutes. Once all the water has evaporated, stir-fry for 2 minutes and set aside.

4 Meanwhile, place the rice in a pan. Add the cumin seeds, cardamoms, remaining salt, and enough water for cooking, and cook over medium heat until the rice is half cooked. Drain. Remove half of the rice and place in a bowl.

5 Spoon the meat mixture on top of the rice in the pan. Add half each of the saffron milk, lemon juice, chilies, and cilantro. Then add the reserved onions and ghee, and the remaining rice, saffron milk, lemon juice, chilies, and cilantro. Cover and cook over low heat for 15–20 minutes, or until the rice is cooked. Stir well and serve hot.

59

roman pan-fried lamb

serves four

1 tbsp oil

1 tbsp butter

1 lb 5 oz/600 g lamb, shoulder
or leg, cut into 1-inch/
2.5-cm chunks

4 garlic cloves, peeled

3 fresh thyme sprigs, stems removed

6 canned anchovies

⅔ cup red wine

⅔ cup lamb stock

1 tsp sugar

generous ¼ cup black olives, pitted
and halved

2 tbsp chopped fresh parsley,
to garnish

mashed potatoes, to serve

COOK'S TIP

Rome is the capital of both Italy
and the region of Lazio and thus
has become a focal point for
specialties from all over Italy.
Food from this region tends to
be fairly simple and quick to
prepare, with plenty of herbs
and seasonings giving really
robust flavors.

1 Heat the oil and butter in a large skillet. Add the lamb and cook for 4–5 minutes, stirring, until the meat is browned all over.

2 Using a mortar and pestle, grind together the garlic, thyme, and anchovies to make a smooth paste.

3 Add the wine and stock to the skillet, then stir in the garlic and anchovy paste together with the sugar.

4 Bring the mixture to a boil, then reduce the heat and let simmer, covered, for 30–40 minutes, or until the lamb is tender. For the last 10 minutes of the cooking time, remove the lid in order to let the sauce reduce slightly.

5 Stir the olives into the sauce and mix to combine.

6 Transfer the lamb and the sauce to a serving bowl and garnish with parsley. Serve with creamy mashed potatoes.

lamb curry in a thick sauce

serves six

2 lb 4 oz/1 kg lean lamb

generous ⅓ cup plain yogurt

½ cup almonds

2 tsp garam masala

2 tsp finely chopped fresh
    gingerroot

2 garlic cloves, crushed

1½ tsp chili powder

1½ tsp salt

1¼ cups oil

3 onions, finely chopped

4 green cardamoms

2 bay leaves

3 fresh green chilies, chopped

2 tbsp lemon juice

14 oz/400 g canned tomatoes

1¼ cups water

1 small bunch cilantro, chopped

boiled rice, to serve

1 Using a very sharp knife, cut the lamb into small, even-size pieces.

2 In a large mixing bowl, combine the yogurt, almonds, garam masala, ginger, garlic, chili powder, and salt, stirring to mix well.

3 Heat the oil in a large pan and sauté the onions with the cardamoms and the bay leaves until golden brown, stirring constantly.

4 Add the meat and the yogurt mixture to the pan and stir-fry for 3–5 minutes.

5 Add 2 of the chilies, the lemon juice, and tomatoes to the mixture in the pan and stir-fry for an additional 5 minutes.

6 Add the water to the pan, then cover and let simmer over low heat for 35–40 minutes.

7 Add the remaining chili and the cilantro and stir until the sauce has thickened. (Remove the lid and increase the heat if the sauce is too watery.)

8 Transfer the curry to warmed serving plates and serve hot with boiled rice.

simmered medley

serves six–eight

2 lb/900 g boneless pork

2 bay leaves

1 onion, chopped

8 garlic cloves, finely chopped

2 tbsp chopped cilantro

1 carrot, thinly sliced

2 celery stalks, diced

2 chicken bouillon cubes

½ chicken, cut into portions

4–5 ripe tomatoes, diced

½ tsp mild chili powder

grated rind of ¼ orange

¼ tsp ground cumin

juice of 3 oranges

1 zucchini, cut into
    bite-size pieces

¼ cabbage, thinly sliced
    and blanched

1 apple, cut into bite-size pieces

about 10 prunes, pitted

¼ tsp ground cinnamon

pinch of ground ginger

2 hard chorizo sausages, about
    12 oz/350 g in total, cut into
    bite-size pieces

salt and pepper

rice, tortillas, and salsa, to serve

1 Combine the pork, bay leaves, onion, garlic, cilantro, carrot, and celery in a large pan and fill with cold water. Bring to a boil, skimming off the scum on the surface. Reduce the heat and let simmer gently for 1 hour.

2 Add the bouillon cubes to the pan with the chicken, tomatoes, chili powder, orange rind, and cumin. Cook for an additional 45 minutes, or until the chicken is tender. Spoon off the fat that forms on the top.

3 Add the orange juice, zucchini, cabbage, apple, prunes, cinnamon, ginger, and chorizo. Let simmer for an additional 20 minutes, or until the zucchini is tender and the chorizo is completely cooked through.

4 Season the stew to taste with salt and pepper. Serve at once with rice, tortillas, and salsa.

fruity lamb casserole

serves four

1 lb/450 g lean lamb, trimmed and
   cut into 1-inch/2.5-cm cubes

1 tsp ground cinnamon

1 tsp ground coriander

1 tsp ground cumin

2 tsp olive oil

1 red onion, finely chopped

1 garlic clove, crushed

14 oz/400 g canned
   chopped tomatoes

2 tbsp tomato paste

salt and pepper

¾ cup no-soak dried apricots

1 tsp superfine sugar

1¼ cups vegetable stock

1 small bunch cilantro, to garnish

brown rice, couscous, or bulgur
   wheat, to serve

1 Preheat the oven to 350°F/180°C. Place the meat in a mixing bowl and add the cinnamon, ground coriander, cumin, and oil. Mix thoroughly so that the lamb is well coated in the spices.

2 Heat a nonstick skillet for a few seconds until it is hot, then add the spiced lamb. Reduce the heat and cook for 4–5 minutes, stirring, until browned all over. Using a slotted spoon, remove the lamb and transfer to a large, ovenproof casserole.

3 Add the onion, garlic, tomatoes, and tomato paste to the skillet and cook, stirring occasionally, for 5 minutes. Season to taste with salt and pepper. Stir in the apricots, sugar, and stock and bring to a boil.

4 Spoon the sauce over the lamb and mix well. Cover and cook in the oven for 1 hour, removing the lid of the casserole for the last 10 minutes.

5 Coarsely chop the cilantro and sprinkle over the casserole to garnish. Serve with brown rice, couscous, or bulgur wheat.

lean lamb cooked in spinach

serves two–four

1¼ cups oil

2 onions, sliced

¼ bunch cilantro, chopped, plus
extra to garnish

3 fresh green chilies, chopped

1½ tsp finely chopped fresh
gingerroot

1–2 garlic cloves, crushed

1 tsp chili powder

½ tsp ground turmeric

1 lb/450 g lean lamb, cubed

1 tsp salt

2 lb 4 oz/1 kg fresh spinach,
chopped, or 15 oz/425 g
canned spinach

3 cups water

fresh gingerroot, shredded,
to garnish

1 Heat the oil in a skillet over medium heat, then add the onions and cook until pale golden.

2 Add the cilantro and 2 of the chilies to the skillet and stir-fry for 3–5 minutes.

3 Reduce the heat and add the ginger, garlic, chili powder, and turmeric to the mixture in the skillet, stirring to mix.

4 Add the lamb to the skillet and stir-fry for an additional 5 minutes. Add the salt and spinach and cook for 3–5 minutes.

5 Add the water, stirring, then cover the skillet and cook over low heat for 45 minutes. Remove the lid and check the meat; if it is not tender, turn the meat over and increase the heat, then cook, uncovered, until the surplus water has been absorbed. Stir-fry the mixture for an additional 5–7 minutes.

6 Transfer the lamb and spinach mixture to a serving dish and garnish with shredded ginger, cilantro, and the remaining chopped chili. Serve hot.

potatoes cooked with meat & yogurt

serves six

3 potatoes

1¼ cups oil

3 onions, sliced

2 lb 4 oz/1 kg leg of lamb, cubed

2 tsp garam masala

1½ tsp finely chopped fresh
   gingerroot

1–2 garlic cloves, crushed

1 tsp chili powder

3 black peppercorns

3 green cardamoms

1 tsp black cumin seeds

2 cinnamon sticks

1 tsp paprika

1½ tsp salt

⅔ cup plain yogurt

2½ cups water

TO GARNISH

2 fresh green chilies, chopped

cilantro, chopped

1 Peel and cut each potato into
6 pieces.

2 Heat the oil in a pan and sauté
the sliced onions until golden
brown. Remove the onions and set
aside until required.

3 Add the meat and half the garam
masala to the pan and stir-fry for
5–7 minutes over low heat.

4 Return the cooked onions to
the pan and remove from
the heat.

5 In a small bowl, mix together
the remaining garam masala
and the ginger, garlic, chili powder,
peppercorns, cardamoms, cumin seeds,
cinnamon sticks, paprika, and salt.
Add the yogurt and mix well.

6 Return the pan to the heat and
gradually add the spice and
yogurt mixture to the meat and onions,
then stir-fry for 7–10 minutes. Add the
water and reduce the heat, then cook,
covered, for 40 minutes, stirring
occasionally.

7 Add the potatoes to the pan and
cook, covered, for an additional
15 minutes, gently stirring the mixture
occasionally. Garnish with chilies and
cilantro and serve at once.

azerbaijani lamb pilaf

serves four–six

2–3 tbsp vegetable oil

1 lb 7 oz/650 g boneless lamb
  shoulder, cut into 1-inch/
  2.5-cm cubes

2 onions, coarsely chopped

1 tsp ground cumin

1 cup risotto, long-grain, or
  basmati rice

1 tbsp tomato paste

1 tsp saffron threads

generous ⅓ cup pomegranate juice
  (see Cook's Tip)

3½ cups lamb or chicken stock,
  or water

⅔ cup no-soak dried apricots or
  prunes, halved

2 tbsp raisins

salt and pepper

TO SERVE

2 tbsp chopped fresh mint

2 tbsp chopped fresh watercress

1 Heat the oil in a large, ovenproof casserole or wide pan over high heat. Add the lamb, in batches, and cook, stirring and turning frequently, for 7 minutes, or until lightly browned.

2 Add the onions and reduce the heat to medium–high, then cook for 2 minutes, or until starting to soften. Add the cumin and rice and cook, stirring to coat, for 2 minutes, or until the rice is translucent. Stir in the tomato paste and the saffron threads.

3 Add the pomegranate juice and stock and bring to a boil, stirring. Stir in the apricots and raisins. Reduce the heat to low, then cover and let simmer for 20–25 minutes, or until the lamb and rice are tender and the liquid is absorbed.

4 To serve, season to taste with salt and pepper, then sprinkle the chopped mint and watercress over the pilaf and serve from the casserole.

COOK'S TIP

Pomegranate juice is available from Middle Eastern grocery stores. If you cannot find it, substitute unsweetened grape or apple juice.

red lamb curry

serves four

1 lb 2 oz/500 g boneless lean leg
   of lamb

2 tbsp vegetable oil

1 large onion, sliced

2 garlic cloves, crushed

2 tbsp red curry paste

⅔ cup coconut milk

1 tbsp brown sugar

1 large red bell pepper, seeded and
   thickly sliced

½ cup lamb or beef stock

1 tbsp Thai fish sauce

2 tbsp lime juice

8 oz/225 g canned water
   chestnuts, drained

2 tbsp chopped cilantro

2 tbsp chopped fresh basil, plus
   extra leaves to garnish

salt and pepper

boiled jasmine rice, to serve

COOK'S TIP

This curry can also be made
with other lean meats.
Try replacing the lamb with
trimmed duck breasts or pieces
of lean rump beef.

1 Trim the meat and cut it into
1¼-inch/3-cm cubes. Heat the oil
in a large skillet or preheated wok over
high heat and stir-fry the onion and
garlic for 2–3 minutes, or until
softened. Add the meat and stir-fry
until lightly browned.

2 Stir in the curry paste and cook
for a few seconds, then add the
coconut milk and sugar and bring to
a boil. Reduce the heat and let simmer
for 15 minutes, stirring occasionally.

3 Stir in the bell pepper, stock,
fish sauce, and lime juice.
Cover and let simmer for an additional
15 minutes, or until the meat is tender.

4 Add the water chestnuts, cilantro,
and basil and adjust the
seasoning to taste. Serve, garnished
with basil leaves, with jasmine rice.

Chicken

Chicken is the perfect choice for one-pot cooking because there are so many different cuts, from inexpensive thighs to delicate breast  meat, as well as the whole bird. In addition, as it is often rather bland in flavor, it benefits from being combined with vegetables, fruit, herbs, and aromatics. Almost everyone loves chicken, and the recipes in this chapter reflect its universal popularity, with dishes from many countries, including Mexico, India, Thailand, Spain, Italy, and the Middle East. It is a versatile meat and can be cooked in any number of ways, from casseroles to stir-fries and from risottos to curries. There are recipes for all occasions and every time of year, from Sunday lunch with the family to an alfresco dinner party. Hot and spicy, rich and creamy, filling and flavorsome, subtle and delicate—there is a one-pot chicken dish that is sure to please.

chicken & chickpea soup

serves four

2 tbsp butter

3 scallions, chopped

2 garlic cloves, crushed

1 fresh marjoram sprig,
    finely chopped

12 oz/350 g skinless, boneless
    chicken breasts, diced

5 cups chicken stock

12 oz/350 g canned
    chickpeas, drained

1 bouquet garni

salt and pepper

1 red bell pepper, seeded and diced

1 green bell pepper, seeded
    and diced

4 oz/115 g small dried pasta shapes

croutons, to serve

1 Melt the butter in a large pan over medium heat. Add the scallions, garlic, marjoram, and chicken and cook, stirring frequently, for 5 minutes.

2 Add the stock, chickpeas, and bouquet garni and season to taste with salt and pepper.

3 Bring the soup to a boil, then reduce the heat and let simmer for 2 hours.

4 Add the bell peppers and pasta to the pan, then let simmer for an additional 20 minutes.

5 To serve, ladle the soup into individual serving bowls and serve at once, garnished with croutons.

COOK'S TIP

If you prefer, use dried chickpeas. Cover with cold water and set aside to soak for 5–8 hours. Drain and add the beans to the soup, according to the recipe, and allow an additional 30 minutes–1 hour cooking time.

lemon & chicken soup

serves four

4 tbsp butter

8 shallots, thinly sliced

2 carrots, thinly sliced

2 celery stalks, thinly sliced

8 oz/225 g skinless, boneless
chicken breasts, finely chopped

3 lemons

5 cups chicken stock

8 oz/225 g dried spaghetti, broken
into small pieces

salt and pepper

⅔ cup heavy cream

TO GARNISH

fresh parsley sprigs

2 lemon slices, halved

COOK'S TIP

You can prepare this soup in
advance up to the end of Step 3,
so that all you need do before
serving is heat it through very
gently before adding the pasta
and the finishing touches.

1 Melt the butter in a large pan.
Add the shallots, carrots, celery,
and chicken and cook over low heat,
stirring occasionally, for 8 minutes.

2 Thinly pare the lemons and
blanch the lemon rind in boiling
water for 3 minutes. Squeeze the juice
from the lemons.

3 Add the lemon rind and juice to
the pan, together with the stock.
Bring the soup slowly to a boil over
low heat and let simmer for
40 minutes, stirring occasionally.

4 Add the spaghetti to the pan and
cook for 15 minutes. Season to
taste with salt and pepper and add the
cream. Heat through, but do not let the
soup boil, or it will curdle.

5 Pour the soup into individual
bowls and garnish with parsley
and half slices of lemon, then serve
at once.

chicken & asparagus soup

serves four

8 oz/225 g asparagus

3½ cups chicken stock

⅔ cup dry white wine

1 sprig each of fresh parsley, dill,
and tarragon

1 garlic clove

2 oz/55 g dried vermicelli
rice noodles

12 oz/350 g lean cooked chicken,
finely shredded

salt and pepper

1 small leek, to garnish

COOK'S TIP

Rice noodles contain no fat
and are an ideal substitute for
egg noodles.

---

1 Wash the asparagus and trim away the woody ends. Cut each spear into pieces 1½ inches/4 cm long.

2 Pour the chicken stock and wine into a large pan and bring to a boil.

3 Wash the herbs and tie them together with clean string. Peel the garlic clove and add to the pan with the herbs, asparagus, and noodles. Cover and let simmer for 5 minutes.

4 Stir in the chicken and season well with salt and pepper. Let simmer gently for an additional 3–4 minutes, or until heated through.

5 Trim the leek, then slice it down the center and wash under cold running water to remove any dirt. Shake dry and finely shred.

6 Remove the herbs and garlic from the pan and discard. Ladle the soup into warmed bowls and sprinkle with shredded leek. Serve at once.

VARIATION

You can use any of your favorite
herbs in this recipe, but choose
those with a subtle flavor so that
they do not overpower the
asparagus. Small, tender
asparagus spears give the best
results and flavor.

chicken, avocado & chipotle soup

serves four

generous 6⅓ cups chicken stock

2–3 garlic cloves, finely chopped

1–2 dried chipotle chilies,
reconstituted and cut into very
thin strips (see Cook's Tip)

1 avocado

lime or lemon juice, for tossing

3–5 scallions, thinly sliced

12–14 oz/350–400 g cooked
chicken breast meat, shredded

2 tbsp chopped fresh cilantro

TO SERVE

1 lime, cut into wedges

handful of tortilla chips (optional)

COOK'S TIP

Chipotle chilies are smoked and dried jalapeño chilies, available canned or dried from specialty stores. Use chipotles canned in adobo marinade (drained) for this recipe, if possible. Dried chipotles need to be reconstituted before using—place in a heatproof bowl, then pour over boiling water and let stand for 1–2 hours, or until softened.

1 Place the stock in a large, heavy-bottom pan with the garlic and chilies and bring to a boil.

2 Meanwhile, cut the avocado in half around the pit. Twist apart, then remove the pit with a knife. Carefully peel off the skin and dice the flesh, then toss in lime or lemon juice to prevent discoloration.

3 Arrange the scallions, chicken, avocado, and cilantro in the base of 4 soup bowls or in a large serving bowl.

4 Ladle hot stock over and serve with lime wedges and a handful of tortilla chips, if wished.

chicken, noodle & corn soup

serves four

1 lb/450 g skinless, boneless
    chicken breasts, cut into strips

5 cups chicken stock

⅔ cup heavy cream

salt and pepper

3½ oz/100 g dried vermicelli

1 tbsp cornstarch

3 tbsp milk

¾ cup corn kernels

1 Put the chicken, stock, and cream into a large pan and bring to a boil over low heat. Reduce the heat slightly and let simmer for 20 minutes. Season the soup to taste with salt and pepper.

2 Meanwhile, cook the vermicelli in lightly salted boiling water for 10–12 minutes, or until just tender. Drain the pasta and keep warm.

3 In a small bowl, mix together the cornstarch and milk to make a smooth paste. Stir the cornstarch into the soup until thickened.

4 Add the corn and vermicelli to the pan and heat through.

5 Transfer the soup to warmed individual soup bowls and serve.

VARIATION

For crab and corn soup, substitute 1 lb/450 g cooked crabmeat for the chicken breasts. Flake the crabmeat well before adding it to the pan and reduce the cooking time by 10 minutes.

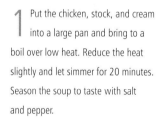

chicken, corn & bean soup

serves six

1½ tbsp butter

1 large onion, finely chopped

1 garlic clove, finely chopped

3 tbsp all-purpose flour

2½ cups water

4 cups chicken stock

1 carrot, cut into fourths and
  thinly sliced

6 oz/175 g green beans, trimmed
  and cut into short pieces

14 oz/400 g canned lima beans,
  rinsed and drained

2 cups cooked or frozen corn kernels

8 oz/225 g cooked chicken meat

salt and pepper

VARIATION

Replace the canned lima beans
with generous 3 cups cooked
fresh fava beans, peeled if
wished. You could also substitute
sliced string beans for
the green beans.

1 Melt the butter in a large pan over medium–low heat. Add the onion and garlic and cook, stirring frequently, for 3–4 minutes, or until just softened.

2 Stir in the flour and cook for an additional 2 minutes, stirring occasionally.

3 Gradually pour in the water, stirring constantly and scraping the bottom of the pan to mix in the flour. Bring to a boil, stirring frequently, and cook for 2 minutes. Add the stock and stir until smooth.

4 Add the carrot, green beans, lima beans, corn, and chicken. Season to taste with salt and pepper. Return to the boil, then reduce the heat to medium–low and let simmer, covered, for 35 minutes, or until the vegetables are tender.

5 Taste the soup and adjust the seasoning, adding salt, if needed, and plenty of pepper.

6 Ladle the soup into warmed bowls and serve.

chicken jalfrezi

serves four

1 tsp mustard oil

3 tbsp vegetable oil

1 large onion, finely chopped

3 garlic cloves, crushed

1 tbsp tomato paste

2 tomatoes, peeled and chopped

1 tsp ground turmeric

½ tsp cumin seeds, ground

½ tsp coriander seeds, ground

½ tsp chili powder

½ tsp garam masala

1 tsp red wine vinegar

1 small red bell pepper, seeded
    and chopped

1 cup frozen fava beans

1 lb/450 g cooked chicken breasts,
    cut into bite-size pieces

salt

cilantro sprigs, to garnish

1 Heat the mustard oil in a large skillet set over high heat for 1 minute, or until it starts to smoke. Add the vegetable oil, then reduce the heat, add the onion and garlic, and sauté until golden.

2 Add the tomato paste, tomatoes, turmeric, cumin, coriander, chili powder, garam masala, and vinegar to the skillet. Stir until fragrant.

3 Add the bell pepper and fava beans and stir for 2 minutes, or until the bell pepper is softened. Stir in the chicken and season to taste with salt. Let simmer gently for 6–8 minutes, or until the chicken is heated through and the beans are tender.

4 Serve the chicken, garnished with cilantro sprigs.

COOK'S TIP

This dish is an ideal way of making use of leftover cooked poultry or game birds—turkey, duck, or quail. Any variety of beans works well, or substitute root vegetables, zucchini, potatoes, or broccoli. Leafy vegetables will not be so successful.

spiced chicken casserole

serves four–six

3 tbsp olive oil

2 lb/900 g chicken, sliced

10 shallots

3 carrots, chopped

2 oz/55 g chestnuts, sliced

½ cup slivered almonds, toasted

1 tsp freshly grated nutmeg

3 tsp ground cinnamon

1¼ cups white wine

1¼ cups chicken stock

¾ cup white wine vinegar

1 tbsp chopped fresh tarragon

1 tbsp chopped fresh parsley

1 tbsp chopped fresh thyme

grated rind of 1 orange

1 tbsp brown sugar

salt and pepper

scant ¾ cup seedless black
   grapes, halved

fresh herbs, to garnish

freshly cooked wild rice, to serve

COOK'S TIP

This casserole would also be
delicious served with thick slices
of crusty whole-wheat bread to
soak up the sauce.

1 Heat the oil in a large, heavy-bottom pan. Add the chicken, shallots and carrots and sauté for 6 minutes, or until browned.

2 Add the remaining ingredients, except the grapes, and let simmer over low heat for 2 hours, or until the meat is very tender. Stir occasionally.

3 Add the grapes just before serving. Transfer to individual plates and garnish with fresh herbs. Serve with freshly cooked wild rice.

chicken & noodle one-pot

serves four

1 tbsp corn oil

1 onion, sliced

1 garlic clove, crushed

1-inch/2.5-cm piece fresh
    gingerroot, grated

1 bunch scallions,
    diagonally sliced

1 lb 2 oz/500 g skinless, boneless
    chicken breasts, cut into
    bite-size pieces

2 tbsp mild curry paste

2 cups coconut milk

1¼ cups chicken stock

salt and pepper

9 oz/250 g dried Chinese
    egg noodles

2 tsp lime juice

fresh basil sprigs, to garnish

COOK'S TIP

If you enjoy hot flavors,
substitute the mild curry paste in
the above recipe with hot curry
paste (found in most
supermarkets), but reduce the
quantity to 1 tablespoon.

1 Heat the oil in a preheated wok
or large, heavy-bottom skillet.

2 Add the onion, garlic, ginger,
and scallions and stir-fry over
medium heat for 2 minutes, or
until softened.

3 Add the chicken and curry paste
and stir-fry for 4 minutes, or until
the vegetables and chicken are golden
brown. Stir in the coconut milk, stock,
and salt and pepper to taste and
mix well.

4 Bring to a boil, then break
the noodles into large pieces,
if necessary, and add to the wok.
Cover and let simmer, stirring
occasionally, for 6–8 minutes, or until
the noodles are just tender.

5 Add the lime juice and adjust the
seasoning if necessary.

6 Serve the Chicken and Noodle
One-Pot at once in warmed
deep soup bowls, garnished with
basil sprigs.

tom's toad-in-the-hole

serves four–six

generous ¾ cup all-purpose flour

pinch of salt

1 egg, beaten

scant 1 cup milk

⅓ cup water

2 tbsp beef drippings

9 oz/250 g skinless, boneless
    chicken breasts

9 oz/250 g Cumberland sausage

VARIATION

Use skinless, boneless chicken
legs instead of chicken breast in
the recipe. Cut up as directed.
Instead of Cumberland sausage,
use your favorite variety
of sausage.

1 Mix the flour and salt in a bowl,
then make a well in the center
and add the beaten egg.

2 Add half the milk and, using
a wooden spoon, work in the
flour slowly.

3 Beat the mixture until smooth,
then gradually add the remaining
milk and water.

4 Beat again until the mixture is
smooth. Let the mixture stand for
at least 1 hour.

5 Preheat the oven to 425°F/220°C.
Add the drippings to individual
baking pans or to 1 large baking pan.
Cut up the chicken and sausage so that
you get a generous piece in each
individual pan or several scattered
around the large pan.

6 Heat in the oven for 5 minutes,
or until very hot. Remove the pans
from the oven and pour in the batter.

7 Return to the oven to cook for
35 minutes, or until risen and
golden brown. Do not open the oven
door for at least 30 minutes. Serve hot.

chicken pepperonata

serves four

8 chicken thighs

2 tbsp whole-wheat flour

2 tbsp olive oil

1 small onion, thinly sliced

1 garlic clove, crushed

1 each large red, yellow, and
    green bell pepper, seeded and
    thinly sliced

14 oz/400 g canned
    chopped tomatoes

1 tbsp chopped fresh oregano,
    plus extra to garnish

salt and pepper

crusty whole-wheat bread, to serve

COOK'S TIP

If you do not have fresh oregano, use canned tomatoes with herbs already added. For extra flavor, halve the bell peppers and broil under a preheated broiler until the skins are charred. Let cool, then remove the skins and seeds. Slice the bell peppers thinly and use in the recipe.

1 Remove the skin from the chicken thighs and toss in the flour.

2 Heat the oil in a wide skillet. Add the chicken and sauté quickly until sealed and lightly browned, then remove from the skillet. Add the onion to the skillet and gently cook until soft. Add the garlic, bell peppers, tomatoes, and oregano, then bring to a boil, stirring constantly.

3 Arrange the chicken over the vegetable mixture and season well with salt and pepper, then cover the skillet tightly and let simmer for 20–25 minutes, or until the chicken is tender and the juices run clear when a skewer is inserted into the thickest part of the meat.

4 Taste and adjust the seasoning, if necessary. Garnish with oregano and serve with slices of crusty whole-wheat bread.

karahi chicken

serves four

2 tbsp ghee or oil

3 garlic cloves, crushed

1 onion, finely chopped

2 tbsp garam masala

1 tsp coriander seeds, ground

½ tsp dried mint

1 bay leaf

1 lb 10 oz/750 g skinless, boneless chicken, diced

scant 1 cup chicken stock

1 tbsp chopped cilantro

salt

warmed naan bread or chapatis, to serve

1 Heat the ghee in a karahi, wok, or a large, heavy-bottom skillet. Add the garlic and onion and stir-fry for 4 minutes, or until the onion is golden.

2 Stir in the garam masala, ground coriander, mint, and bay leaf.

3 Add the chicken and cook over high heat, stirring occasionally, for 5 minutes. Add the stock, then reduce the heat and let simmer for 10 minutes, or until the sauce has thickened, the chicken is tender, and the juices run clear when a skewer is inserted into the thickest part of the meat.

4 Stir in the chopped cilantro and season to taste with salt, then mix well. Serve at once with warmed naan bread or chapatis.

COOK'S TIP

It is important always to heat a karahi or wok before you add the oil to help maintain the high temperature.

chicken tikka

serves six

1 tsp finely chopped fresh
   gingerroot

1 garlic clove, crushed

½ tsp ground coriander

½ tsp ground cumin

1 tsp chili powder

3 tbsp plain yogurt

1 tsp salt

2 tbsp lemon juice

few drops of red food coloring
   (optional)

1 tbsp tomato paste

3 lb 5 oz/1.5 kg skinless, boneless
   chicken breasts

1 onion, sliced

3 tbsp oil

1 lemon, cut into wedges,
   to garnish

12 lettuce leaves, to serve

1 Blend together the ginger, garlic, coriander, cumin, and chili powder in a large mixing bowl.

2 Add the yogurt, salt, lemon juice, red food coloring, if using, and the tomato paste to the spice mixture.

3 Using a sharp knife, cut the chicken into pieces. Add the chicken to the spice mixture and toss to coat well. Cover and let marinate in the refrigerator for at least 3 hours, preferably overnight.

4 Preheat the broiler. Arrange the onion in the bottom of an ovenproof dish. Carefully drizzle half the oil over the onion.

5 Arrange the marinated chicken pieces on top of the onions and cook under the hot broiler, turning once and basting with the remaining oil, for 25–30 minutes.

6 Serve on a bed of lettuce, garnished with lemon wedges.

COOK'S TIP

Serve the Chicken Tikka with
warmed naan bread, cucumber
raita, and an Indian chutney,
such as mango.

fricassée of chicken in lime sauce

serves four

1 large chicken, cut into
small portions

generous ⅓ cup flour, seasoned

2 tbsp corn oil

1 lb 2 oz/500 g pearl onions or
shallots, sliced

1 each green and red bell pepper,
seeded and thinly sliced

⅔ cup chicken stock

grated rind and juice of 2 limes

2 fresh chilies, chopped

2 tbsp oyster sauce

1 tsp Worcestershire sauce

salt and pepper

VARIATION

Try this casserole with cheese
biscuits. About 30 minutes
before the end of cooking time,
simply top with circles cut from
cheese biscuit pie dough.

1 Preheat the oven to 375°F/190°C.
Coat the chicken pieces in the
seasoned flour. Heat the oil in a
large skillet, then add the chicken and
cook for 4 minutes, or until browned
all over.

2 Using a slotted spoon, transfer
the chicken to a large, deep
casserole and sprinkle with the sliced
onions. Keep warm until required.

3 Slowly cook the bell peppers in
the juices remaining in the skillet.
Add the stock and lime rind and juice
and cook for an additional 5 minutes.

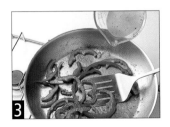

4 Add the chilies, oyster sauce, and
Worcestershire sauce. Season to
taste with salt and pepper.

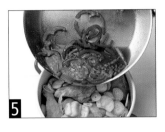

5 Pour the bell peppers and juices
over the chicken and onions.

6 Cover the casserole with a lid
or foil.

7 Cook in the center of the oven for
1½ hours, or until the chicken is
very tender, then serve.

springtime chicken cobbler

serves four

1 tbsp oil

8 skinless chicken drumsticks

1 small onion, sliced

12 oz/350 g baby carrots

2 baby turnips

generous 1 cup fresh or frozen peas

1 tsp cornstarch

1¼ cups chicken stock

2 bay leaves

salt and pepper

COBBLER TOPPING

scant 2 cups whole-wheat flour,
    plus extra for dusting

2 tsp baking powder

2 tbsp sunflower soft margarine

2 tsp dry mustard

2 oz/55 g Cheddar cheese, grated

2–3 tbsp skim milk, plus extra
    for brushing

sesame seeds, for sprinkling

1 Preheat the oven to 400°F/200°C. Heat the oil in a large, ovenproof casserole. Add the chicken and cook, turning frequently, until golden brown. Drain well and remove. Add the onion to the casserole and sauté for 2–3 minutes, or until softened.

2 Cut the carrots and turnips into equal-size pieces. Add to the casserole with the onion, peas, and chicken.

3 Blend the cornstarch with a little of the stock in a small pan, then stir in the remainder and heat gently, stirring, until boiling. Pour into the casserole and add the bay leaves and salt and pepper to taste. Cover the casserole and bake in the oven for 50–60 minutes, or until the chicken is tender and the juices run clear when a skewer is inserted into the thickest part of the meat.

4 For the topping, sift the flour and baking powder into a large bowl, then mix in the margarine with a fork. Stir in the mustard, cheese, and enough milk to form a fairly soft dough. Roll out on a floured counter. Cut out 16 circles with a 1½-inch/4-cm cutter. Uncover the casserole and arrange the circles on top. Brush with milk and sprinkle with sesame seeds. Bake for an additional 20 minutes, or until the topping is golden and firm.

chicken basquaise

serves four–five

1 chicken, weighing 3 lb/1.3 kg,
    cut into 8 pieces
flour, for coating
salt and pepper
3 tbsp olive oil
1 Spanish onion, thickly sliced
2 red, green, or yellow bell peppers,
    seeded and cut lengthwise into
    thick strips
2 garlic cloves
5 oz/140 g chorizo sausage,
    skinned and cut into ½-inch/
    1-cm pieces
1 tbsp tomato paste
1 cup long-grain white rice
2 cups chicken stock
1 tsp crushed dried chilies
½ tsp dried thyme
4 oz/115 g Bayonne or other air-
    dried ham, diced
12 dry-cured black olives
2 tbsp chopped fresh
    flatleaf parsley

1 Pat the chicken pieces dry with paper towels. Put 2 tablespoons of flour in a plastic bag and season well with salt and pepper, then add the chicken pieces. Seal the bag and shake to coat the chicken.

2 Heat 2 tablespoons of the oil in a large, ovenproof casserole over medium–high heat. Add the chicken and cook, turning frequently, for 15 minutes, or until well browned all over. Transfer to a plate.

3 Heat the remaining oil in the casserole and add the onion and bell peppers. Reduce the heat to medium and stir-fry until starting to color and soften. Add the garlic, chorizo, and tomato paste and cook, stirring constantly, for about 3 minutes. Add the rice and cook, stirring to coat, for 2 minutes, or until the rice is translucent.

4 Add the stock, crushed chilies, and thyme, then season to taste with salt and pepper, and stir well. Bring to a boil. Return the chicken to the casserole, pressing it gently into the rice. Cover and cook over very low heat for 45 minutes, or until the chicken is cooked through and the rice is tender.

5 Gently stir the ham, black olives, and half the parsley into the rice mixture. Cover and heat through for an additional 5 minutes. Sprinkle with the remaining parsley and serve at once.

chicken & onions

serves four

1¼ cups oil

4 onions, finely chopped

1½ tsp finely chopped fresh
  gingerroot

1½ tsp garam masala

1 garlic clove, crushed

1 tsp chili powder

1 tsp ground coriander

3 green cardamoms

3 peppercorns

3 tbsp tomato paste

8 chicken thighs, skinned

1¼ cups water

2 tbsp lemon juice

1 fresh green chili, finely chopped

¼ bunch cilantro leaves, chopped

1 fresh green chili, cut into strips,
  to garnish

1 Heat the oil in a large skillet. Add the onions and sauté, stirring occasionally, until golden brown.

2 Reduce the heat and add the ginger, garam masala, garlic, chili powder, ground coriander, cardamoms, and the peppercorns, stirring to mix.

3 Add the tomato paste to the mixture in the skillet and stir-fry for 5–7 minutes.

4 Add the chicken thighs to the skillet and toss to coat with the spice mixture.

5 Pour the water into the skillet, then cover and let simmer for 20–25 minutes.

6 Add the lemon juice, chopped chili, and cilantro to the mixture, and stir to combine.

7 Transfer the chicken and onions to serving plates. Garnish with chili strips and serve hot.

COOK'S TIP

This curry definitely improves
if it is made in advance and
then reheated before serving.
This develops and deepens
the flavors.

chicken bourguignonne

serves four–six

4 tbsp corn oil

2 lb/900 g skinless chicken, diced

9 oz/250 g white mushrooms

4½ oz/125 g rindless smoked
   bacon, diced

16 shallots

2 garlic cloves, crushed

1 tbsp all-purpose flour

⅔ cup white Burgundy wine

⅔ cup chicken stock

1 bouquet garni (1 bay leaf,
   1 fresh thyme sprig, 1 celery
   stalk, 1 fresh parsley sprig, and
   1 fresh sage sprig, tied
   together with string)

salt and pepper

TO SERVE

croutons

selection of cooked vegetables

1 Preheat the oven to 300°F/150°C. Heat the oil in an ovenproof casserole. Add the chicken and cook until browned all over. Remove from the casserole with a slotted spoon and set aside.

2 Add the mushrooms, bacon, shallots, and garlic to the casserole and cook for 4 minutes.

3 Return the chicken to the casserole and sprinkle with flour. Cook for an additional 2 minutes, stirring. Add the wine and stock and bring to a boil, stirring constantly. Add the bouquet garni and season well with salt and pepper.

4 Cover the casserole and bake in the center of the oven for 1½ hours. Remove and discard the bouquet garni.

5 Serve garnished with croutons and accompanied by a selection of lightly cooked vegetables.

COOK'S TIP

A good quality red wine can be
used instead of the white wine,
to produce a rich, glossy
red sauce.

rustic chicken & orange pot

serves four

8 chicken drumsticks, skinned

1 tbsp whole-wheat flour

2 tbsp olive oil

2 red onions

1 garlic clove, crushed

1 tsp fennel seeds

1 bay leaf

finely grated rind and juice of
   1 small orange

14 oz/400 g canned
   chopped tomatoes

14 oz/400 g canned cannellini
   beans or flageolets, drained

salt and pepper

TOPPING

3 thick slices whole-wheat bread

2 tsp olive oil

1 Preheat the oven to 375°F/190°C. Toss the chicken drumsticks in the flour to coat evenly. Heat half the oil in a large, ovenproof casserole. Add the chicken and cook over fairly high heat, turning frequently, until golden brown. Transfer to a plate and keep warm until required.

2 Slice the onions into thin wedges. Heat the remaining oil in the casserole and cook the onions until lightly browned. Stir in the garlic.

3 Add the fennel seeds, bay leaf, orange rind and juice, tomatoes, and beans and season to taste with salt and pepper. Add the chicken.

4 Cover tightly and cook in the oven for 30–35 minutes, or until the chicken is tender and the juices run clear when a skewer is inserted into the thickest part of the meat.

5 Cut the bread into small dice and toss in the oil. Remove the lid from the casserole and top with the bread cubes. Bake for an additional 15–20 minutes, or until the bread is golden and crisp. Serve hot.

COOK'S TIP

Choose beans that are canned in water with no added sugar or salt. Drain and rinse well before use.

chicken & chili bean pot

serves four

2 tbsp all-purpose flour

1 tsp chili powder

salt and pepper

8 chicken thighs or 4 chicken legs

3 tbsp vegetable oil

2 garlic cloves, crushed

1 large onion, chopped

1 green or red bell pepper, seeded
and chopped

1¼ cups chicken stock

12 oz/350 g tomatoes, chopped

14 oz/400 g canned red kidney
beans, rinsed and drained

2 tbsp tomato paste

COOK'S TIP

For extra flavor, use sun-dried
tomato paste instead of
ordinary tomato paste.

1 Combine the flour and chili powder in a shallow dish and add salt and pepper to taste. Rinse the chicken, but do not dry. Dip the chicken into the seasoned flour, turning to coat it on all sides.

2 Heat the oil in a large, deep skillet or ovenproof casserole and add the chicken. Cook over high heat, turning the pieces frequently, for 3–4 minutes, or until browned all over.

3 Lift the chicken out of the skillet with a slotted spoon and drain thoroughly on paper towels.

4 Add the garlic, onion, and bell pepper to the skillet and cook over medium heat, stirring occasionally, for 2–3 minutes, or until softened.

5 Add the stock, tomatoes, beans, and tomato paste, stirring well. Bring to a boil, then return the chicken to the skillet. Reduce the heat, then cover and let simmer for 30 minutes, or until the chicken is tender and the juices run clear when a skewer is inserted into the thickest part of the meat. Taste and adjust the seasoning, if necessary, and serve.

chicken korma

serves eight

1½ tsp finely chopped fresh
   gingerroot

1–2 garlic cloves, crushed

2 tsp garam masala

1 tsp chili powder

1 tsp salt

1 tsp black cumin seeds

3 green cardamoms, husks removed
   and seeds crushed

1 tsp ground coriander

1 tsp ground almonds

⅔ cup plain yogurt

8 skinless, boneless chicken breasts

1¼ cups oil

2 onions, sliced

⅔ cup water

¼ bunch cilantro, chopped

2 fresh green chilies, chopped

boiled rice, to serve

1 In a bowl, mix the ginger, garlic, garam masala, chili powder, salt, cumin seeds, cardamoms, ground coriander, and ground almonds with the yogurt.

2 Spoon the yogurt and spice mixture over the chicken breasts and set aside to marinate.

3 Heat the oil in a large skillet. Add the onions to the skillet and sauté until golden brown.

4 Add the chicken breasts to the skillet, stir-frying for 5–7 minutes.

5 Add the water, then cover and let simmer for 20–25 minutes.

VARIATION

Chicken portions may be used instead of breasts, if preferred, and should be cooked for 10 minutes longer.

6 Add the cilantro and chilies. Cook, stirring occasionally, for an additional 10 minutes, or until the chicken is tender and the juices run clear when a skewer is inserted into the thickest part of the meat.

7 Transfer to a serving plate and serve with boiled rice.

hungarian chicken goulash

serves six

2 lb/900 g chicken, diced

generous ⅓ cup flour, seasoned with
  1 tsp paprika, salt, and pepper

2 tbsp olive oil

2 tbsp butter

1 onion, sliced

24 shallots

1 each red and green bell pepper,
  seeded and chopped

1 tbsp paprika

1 tsp fresh rosemary, crushed

4 tbsp tomato paste

1¼ cups chicken stock

⅔ cup Bordeaux red wine

14 oz/400 g canned
  chopped tomatoes

TO GARNISH

⅔ cup sour cream

1 tbsp chopped fresh parsley

TO SERVE

crusty bread

crisp salad

1 Preheat the oven to 325°F/160°C. Toss the diced chicken in the seasoned flour until it is coated all over.

2 Heat the oil and butter in an ovenproof casserole. Add the onion, shallots, and bell peppers and sauté for 3 minutes.

3 Add the chicken and cook for an additional 4 minutes.

4 Sprinkle with the paprika and crushed rosemary.

5 Add the tomato paste, stock, wine, and tomatoes, then cover and cook the casserole in the center of the oven for 1½ hours, or until the chicken is very tender.

6 Remove the casserole from the oven and let stand for 4 minutes, then garnish with the sour cream and chopped parsley.

7 Serve with chunks of bread and a crisp salad.

VARIATION

Serve the goulash with buttered ribbon noodles instead of bread. For an authentic touch, try a Hungarian red wine instead of the Bordeaux.

chicken risotto à la milanese

serves four

generous ½ cup butter

2 lb/900 g skinless, boneless
   chicken, thinly sliced

1 large onion, chopped

1 lb 2 oz/500 g risotto rice

2½ cups chicken stock

⅔ cup white wine

1 tsp crumbled saffron threads

salt and pepper

fresh flatleaf parsley sprigs,
   to garnish

½ cup freshly grated Parmesan
   cheese, to serve

VARIATION

The possibilities for risotto are
endless—try adding the
following at the end of the
cooking time: cashews and
corn kernels, lightly sautéed
zucchini, and
basil or artichokes and
oyster mushrooms.

1 Heat 2 oz/55 g of the butter in a deep skillet. Add the chicken and onion and sauté until golden brown. Add the rice and stir well, then cook gently for 5 minutes.

2 Heat the stock in a separate pan until boiling, then gradually add to the rice a ladleful at a time. Reserve the last ladleful of stock. Add the wine, saffron, and salt and pepper to taste and mix well. Let simmer gently for 20 minutes, stirring occasionally and adding extra stock if the risotto becomes too dry.

3 Remove the skillet from the heat and let stand for a few minutes. Just before serving, add the reserved stock and simmer for an additional 10 minutes. Transfer the risotto to 4 large serving plates and garnish with the parsley. Serve with the grated Parmesan cheese and remaining butter.

COOK'S TIP

A risotto should have moist but separate grains. Stock should be added a little at a time and only when the previous addition has been completely absorbed.

chicken & potato casserole

serves four

2 tbsp vegetable oil

4 chicken portions, about 8 oz/
   225 g each

2 leeks, sliced

1 garlic clove, crushed

4 tbsp all-purpose flour

3½ cups chicken stock

1¼ cups dry white wine

salt and pepper

4½ oz/125 g baby carrots, halved
   lengthwise

4½ oz/125 g baby corn cobs, halved
   lengthwise

1 lb/450 g small new potatoes

1 fresh or dried bouquet garni

⅔ cup heavy cream

rice, to serve

VARIATION

Use turkey fillets instead of the
chicken, if preferred, and vary
the vegetables according to
those you have to hand.

1 Preheat the oven to 350°F/
180°C. Heat the oil in a large
skillet and cook the chicken, turning,
for 10 minutes, or until browned.
Transfer to a casserole using a
slotted spoon.

2 Add the leeks and garlic and cook
for 2–3 minutes, stirring. Stir in
the flour and cook for another minute.
Remove from the heat and stir in stock,
wine, and salt and pepper to taste.

3 Return the skillet to the heat
and bring to a boil. Stir in the
vegetables and bouquet garni.
Transfer the mixture to the casserole.

4 Cover the casserole and cook in
the oven for 1 hour.

5 Remove the casserole from the
oven and stir in the cream. Return
to the oven, uncovered, and cook for
15 minutes. Remove and discard the
bouquet garni, then taste and adjust
the seasoning. Serve with rice.

chicken braise with rosemary dumplings

serves four

4 chicken quarters

2 tbsp corn oil

2 leeks

9 oz/250 g carrots, chopped

9 oz/250 g parsnips, chopped

2 small turnips, chopped

2½ cups chicken stock

3 tbsp Worcestershire sauce

2 fresh rosemary sprigs

salt and pepper

ROSEMARY DUMPLINGS

scant 1⅓ cups self-rising flour

3½ oz/100 g shredded suet

1 tbsp chopped fresh
   rosemary leaves

salt and pepper

about 2–3 tbsp cold water

1 Remove the skin from the
chicken, if you prefer. Heat the oil
in a large, ovenproof casserole or
heavy-bottom pan. Add the chicken
and cook until golden. Using a slotted
spoon, remove the chicken from the
casserole. Drain off the excess fat.

2 Slice the leeks and add to the
casserole together with the
carrots, parsnips, and turnips. Cook for
5 minutes, or until the vegetables are
lightly colored. Return the chicken to
the casserole.

3 Add the stock, Worcestershire
sauce, and rosemary, and season
to taste with salt and pepper, then
bring to a boil.

4 Reduce the heat, then cover and
let simmer gently for 50 minutes,
or until the chicken is tender and
the juices run clear when a skewer
is inserted into the thickest part of
the meat.

5 To make the dumplings, mix the
flour, suet, rosemary, and salt and
pepper to taste together in a large
bowl. Stir in just enough water to form
a firm dough.

6 Form into 8 small balls between
the palms of your hands and
place on top of the chicken and
vegetables. Cover and let simmer for
an additional 10–12 minutes, or until
the dumplings are well risen. Serve at
once with the casserole.

garlic chicken casserole

serves four

4 tbsp corn oil

2 lb/900 g chicken, chopped

9 oz/250 g mushrooms, sliced

16 shallots

6 garlic cloves, crushed

1 tbsp all-purpose flour

generous 1 cup white wine

generous 1 cup chicken stock

1 bouquet garni (1 bay leaf, 1 fresh
thyme sprig, 1 celery stalk,
1 parsley sprig, and 1 fresh sage
sprig, tied together with string)

salt and pepper

14 oz/400 g canned cranberry
beans

cooked pattypan squash, to serve

1 Preheat the oven to 300°F/150°C. Heat the oil in a large, ovenproof casserole. Add the chicken and cook until browned all over. Remove the chicken from the casserole with a slotted spoon and set aside until required.

2 Add the mushrooms, shallots, and garlic to the casserole and cook for 4 minutes.

3 Return the chicken to the casserole and sprinkle with the flour, then cook for 2 minutes.

4 Add the wine and stock. Stir until boiling, then add the bouquet garni and season well with salt and pepper to taste.

5 Drain the cranberry beans and rinse thoroughly, then add to the casserole.

6 Cover and place in the center of the oven for 2 hours. Remove and discard the bouquet garni and serve the casserole with pattypan squash.

COOK'S TIP

Mushrooms are ideal in a lowfat diet because they are high in flavor and contain no fat. Experiment with the wealth of varieties that are now available from supermarkets. Serve the casserole with brown rice to make this filling dish go even further.

green chicken curry

serves four

6 skinless, boneless chicken thighs

1¾ cups coconut milk

2 garlic cloves, crushed

2 tbsp Thai fish sauce

2 tbsp Thai green curry paste

12 baby eggplants

3 fresh green chilies, finely chopped

3 fresh kaffir lime leaves, shredded, plus extra to garnish (optional)

salt and pepper

4 tbsp chopped cilantro

freshly cooked rice, to serve

1 Cut the chicken into bite-size pieces. Pour the coconut milk into a preheated wok or large skillet over high heat and bring to a boil.

2 Add the chicken, garlic, and fish sauce to the wok and return to a boil. Reduce the heat and let simmer gently for 30 minutes, or until the chicken is just tender.

3 Remove the chicken from the wok with a slotted spoon. Keep warm.

4 Stir the curry paste into the wok, add the eggplant, chilies, and lime leaves and let simmer for 5 minutes.

COOK'S TIP

Baby eggplants, or "pea eggplants" as they are called in Thailand, are traditionally used in this curry, but they are not always available. If you can't find them in an Asian food store, use chopped ordinary eggplant, or substitute a few green peas.

5 Return the chicken to the wok and bring to a boil. Season to taste with salt and pepper, then stir in the cilantro. Transfer to warmed serving plates and garnish with lime leaves, if using, then serve with freshly cooked rice.

sage chicken & rice

serves four

1 large onion, chopped

1 garlic clove, crushed

2 celery stalks, sliced

2 carrots, diced

2 fresh sage sprigs, plus extra
  to garnish

1¼ cups chicken stock

12 oz/350 g skinless, boneless
  chicken breasts

generous 1 cup mixed brown
  and wild rice

14 oz/400 g canned
  chopped tomatoes

dash of Tabasco sauce

salt and pepper

2 zucchini, thinly sliced

3½ oz/100 g lean ham, diced

TO SERVE

salad greens

crusty bread

COOK'S TIP

If you do not have fresh sage,
use 1 teaspoon of dried sage
in Step 1.

---

1 Place the onion, garlic, celery, carrots, and sage in a large pan and pour in the stock. Bring to a boil, then reduce the heat and cover the pan. Let simmer for 5 minutes.

2 Cut the chicken into 1-inch/ 2.5-cm cubes and stir into the pan. Cover and cook for an additional 5 minutes.

3 Stir in the rice and tomatoes, then add Tabasco sauce to taste and season well with salt and pepper. Bring to a boil, then reduce the heat and let simmer, covered, for 25 minutes.

4 Stir in the sliced zucchini and the diced ham and cook, uncovered and stirring occasionally, for an additional 10 minutes, or until the rice is just tender.

5 Remove and discard the sage. Garnish with a few sage leaves and serve with salad greens and slices of crusty bread.

buttered chicken

serves four–six

generous ⅓ cup unsalted butter

1 tbsp oil

2 onions, finely chopped

1 tsp finely chopped fresh
  gingerroot

2 tsp garam masala

2 tsp ground coriander

1 tsp chili powder

1 tsp black cumin seeds

1 garlic clove, crushed

1 tsp salt

3 green cardamoms

3 black peppercorns

⅔ cup plain yogurt

2 tbsp tomato paste

8 chicken pieces, skinned

⅔ cup water

2 bay leaves

⅔ cup light cream

TO GARNISH

chopped cilantro

2 fresh green chilies, chopped

1 Heat the butter and oil in a large skillet over medium heat. Add the onions and sauté, stirring frequently, until golden brown. Reduce the heat.

2 Place the ginger in a bowl. Add the garam masala, ground coriander, chili powder, cumin seeds, garlic, salt, cardamoms, and peppercorns and blend. Add the yogurt and tomato paste and stir to combine.

3 Add the chicken pieces to the yogurt and spice mixture and mix to coat well.

4 Add the chicken to the onions in the skillet and stir-fry vigorously, making semicircular movements, for 5–7 minutes.

5 Add the water and the bay leaves and let simmer for 30 minutes, stirring occasionally.

6 Add the cream and cook for an additional 10–15 minutes.

7 Garnish with cilantro and chilies and serve hot.

brittany chicken casserole

1 lb 2 oz/500 g dried beans, such
    as flageolets, soaked overnight
    and drained

2 tbsp butter

2 tbsp olive oil

3 rindless bacon slices, chopped

2 lb/900 g chicken pieces

1 tbsp all-purpose flour

1¼ cups hard cider

⅔ cup chicken stock

salt and pepper

14 shallots

2 tbsp honey, warmed

8 oz/225 g cooked beet, chopped

1 Preheat the oven to 325°F/160°C. Cook the beans in boiling water for 25 minutes, then drain thoroughly.

2 Heat the butter and oil in a large, ovenproof casserole. Add the bacon and chicken and cook for 5 minutes.

3 Sprinkle with the flour, then add the cider and stock, stirring constantly to avoid lumps forming. Season to taste with salt and pepper and bring to a boil.

4 Add the drained beans, then cover the casserole tightly and bake in the center of the oven for 2 hours, or until the chicken is very tender.

5 About 15 minutes before the end of the cooking time, uncover the casserole.

6 Gently cook the shallots and honey together in a skillet for 5 minutes, turning the shallots frequently until golden.

7 Add the shallots and beet to the casserole and return to the oven for the last 15 minutes of cooking time.

COOK'S TIP

To save time, use canned flageolet beans instead of dried. Rinse and drain before adding to the chicken.

chicken & plum casserole

serves four

2 rindless lean Canadian bacon
   slices, chopped

1 tbsp corn oil

1 lb/450 g skinless, boneless
   chicken thighs, cut into 4 equal-
   size strips

1 garlic clove, crushed

6 oz/175 g shallots, halved

8 oz/225 g plums, halved or
   quartered (if large) and pitted

1 tbsp brown sugar

⅔ cup dry sherry

2 tbsp plum sauce

2 cups chicken stock

2 tsp cornstarch, mixed with 4 tsp
   cold water

2 tbsp chopped fresh parsley,
   to garnish

crusty bread, to serve

VARIATION

Chunks of lean turkey or pork
would also go well with this
combination of flavors.
The cooking time will
remain the same.

1 In a large, nonstick skillet, dry-fry the bacon for 2–3 minutes until the juices run out. Remove the bacon from the skillet with a slotted spoon, set aside, and keep warm.

2 In the same skillet, heat the oil and cook the chicken with the garlic and shallots for 4–5 minutes, stirring occasionally, until well browned all over.

3 Return the bacon to the skillet and stir in the plums, sugar, sherry, plum sauce, and stock. Bring to a boil, then reduce the heat and let simmer for 20 minutes, or until the plums have softened and the chicken is cooked through.

4 Add the cornstarch mixture to the skillet and cook, stirring, for an additional 2–3 minutes, or until thickened.

5 Spoon the casserole onto warmed serving plates and garnish with chopped parsley. Serve with chunks of bread to mop up the fruity gravy.

golden chicken risotto

serves four

2 tbsp corn oil

1 tbsp butter

1 leek, thinly sliced

1 large yellow bell pepper, seeded
and diced

3 skinless, boneless chicken
breasts, diced

generous 1½ cups risotto rice

few saffron threads

salt and pepper

6 cups chicken stock, simmering

7 oz/200 g canned corn kernels

generous ⅓ cup toasted unsalted
peanuts

½ cup freshly grated
Parmesan cheese

COOK'S TIP

Risottos can be frozen, before
adding the Parmesan cheese, for
up to 1 month, but remember to
reheat this risotto thoroughly as
it contains chicken.

1 Heat the oil and butter in a large, heavy-bottom pan. Add the leek and bell pepper and sauté for 1 minute, then stir in the chicken and cook, stirring, until golden brown.

2 Stir in the rice and cook for 2–3 minutes.

3 Stir in the saffron threads and add salt and pepper to taste. Add the stock, a ladleful at a time, then cover and cook over low heat, stirring occasionally, for 20 minutes, or until the rice is tender and most of the liquid is absorbed. Do not let the risotto dry out—add more stock if necessary.

4 Stir in the corn, peanuts, and Parmesan cheese, then taste and adjust the seasoning if necessary. Serve the risotto hot.

tandoori-style chicken

serves four

8 chicken drumsticks, skinned

⅔ cup plain yogurt

1½ tsp finely chopped fresh
  gingerroot

1–2 garlic cloves, crushed

1 tsp chili powder

2 tsp ground cumin

2 tsp ground coriander

1 tsp salt

½ tsp red food coloring

1 tbsp tamarind paste

⅔ cup water

⅔ cup oil

lettuce leaves, to serve

TO GARNISH

onion rings

sliced tomatoes

lemon wedges

1 Make 2–3 slashes in each chicken drumstick.

2 Place the yogurt in a bowl. Add the ginger, garlic, chili powder, cumin, coriander, salt, and red food coloring and blend together until the mixture is well combined.

3 Add the chicken to the yogurt and spice mixture and mix to coat well. Cover and let the chicken marinate in the refrigerator for at least 3 hours.

4 In a separate bowl, mix the tamarind paste with the water and fold into the yogurt and spice mixture. Toss the drumsticks in the mixture and cover. Let marinate in the refrigerator for an additional 3 hours.

5 Preheat the broiler to medium–hot. Transfer the drumsticks to an ovenproof dish and brush with a little oil. Cook, turning the drumsticks occasionally and basting with the remaining oil, for 30–35 minutes, or until tender and the juices run clear when a skewer is inserted into the thickest part of the meat.

6 Arrange the chicken on a bed of lettuce, then garnish with onion rings, tomato slices, and lemon wedges and serve at once.

COOK'S TIP
Serve these succulent chicken pieces with warmed naan bread and a raita.

chicken madeira "french-style"

serves eight

2 tbsp butter

20 shallots

9 oz/250 g carrots, sliced

9 oz/250 g rindless bacon, chopped

9 oz/250 g white mushrooms

1 chicken, weighing 3 lb 5 oz/
   1.5 kg

scant 2 cups white wine

2 tbsp all-purpose flour, seasoned

scant 2 cups chicken stock

salt and pepper

1 bouquet garni sachet

⅔ cup Madeira wine

mashed potatoes, to serve

COOK'S TIP

You can add any combination of herbs to this recipe—chervil is a popular herb in French cuisine, but add it at the end of cooking so that its delicate flavor is not lost. Other herbs that work well with chicken are parsley and tarragon.

1 Heat the butter in a large, ovenproof casserole. Add the shallots, carrots, bacon, and mushrooms and sauté for 3 minutes, stirring frequently. Transfer to a plate and set aside.

2 Add the chicken to the casserole and cook until browned all over. Add the reserved vegetables and bacon to the casserole.

3 Add the white wine and cook until reduced.

4 Sprinkle with the seasoned flour, stirring to avoid lumps forming.

5 Add the stock, salt and pepper to taste, and the bouquet garni. Cover and let simmer for 2 hours, or until the chicken is tender and the juices run clear when a skewer is inserted into the thickest part of the meat. About 30 minutes before the end of the cooking time, add the wine and continue cooking, uncovered.

6 Just before serving, remove and discard the bouquet garni. Carve the chicken and serve with mashed potatoes.

country chicken hotchpotch

serves four

4 chicken quarters

6 potatoes

salt and pepper

2 fresh thyme sprigs

2 fresh rosemary sprigs

2 bay leaves

7 oz/200 g rindless smoked lean
    bacon, diced

1 large onion, finely chopped

7 oz/200 g sliced carrots

⅔ cup stout

2 tbsp melted butter

COOK'S TIP

Serve the hotchpotch with
Rosemary Dumplings (see page
108) for a truly hearty meal.

1 Preheat the oven to
300°F/150°C. Remove the skin
from the chicken quarters, if wished.
Cut the potatoes into ¼-inch/5-mm
thick slices.

2 Arrange a layer of potato slices
in the bottom of a wide casserole.
Season to taste with salt and pepper,
then add the thyme, sprigs of rosemary,
and bay leaves.

3 Top with the chicken quarters,
then sprinkle with the bacon,
onion, and carrots. Season well
with salt and pepper. Arrange the
remaining potato slices over the top,
overlapping slightly.

4 Pour over the stout, brush the
potatoes with the melted butter,
and cover with a lid.

5 Bake in the oven for 2 hours,
uncovering for the last
30 minutes to allow the potatoes
to brown. Serve hot.

country chicken bake

serves four

2 tbsp corn oil

4 chicken quarters

16 small whole onions

3 celery stalks, sliced

14 oz/400 g canned red kidney
  beans, rinsed and drained

4 tomatoes, cut into fourths

scant 1 cup hard cider or
  chicken stock

4 tbsp chopped fresh parsley

salt and pepper

1 tsp paprika

2 oz/55 g butter

12 slices French bread

COOK'S TIP

Add a crushed garlic clove to the
parsley butter for extra flavor.

1 Preheat the oven to 400°F/200°C. Heat the oil in a large, ovenproof casserole. Add the chicken quarters, 2 at a time, and cook until golden. Using a slotted spoon, remove the chicken from the casserole and set aside until required.

2 Add the onions and cook, turning occasionally, until golden brown. Add the celery and cook for 2–3 minutes. Return the chicken to the casserole, then stir in the beans, tomatoes, cider, and half the parsley. Season to taste with salt and pepper and sprinkle with the paprika.

3 Cover and cook in the oven for 20–25 minutes, or until the chicken is tender and the juices run clear when a skewer is inserted into the thickest part of the meat.

4 Mix the remaining parsley and butter together, then spread evenly over the French bread. Uncover the casserole, arrange the bread slices overlapping on top, and bake for an additional 10–12 minutes, or until golden and crisp.

spicy roast chicken

serves four

½ cup ground almonds

⅓ cup dry unsweetened coconut

⅔ cup oil

1 onion, finely chopped

1 tsp chopped fresh gingerroot

1 garlic clove, crushed

1 tsp chili powder

1¼ tsp garam masala

1 tsp salt

⅔ cup plain yogurt

4 chicken quarters, skinned

green salad, to serve

TO GARNISH

chopped cilantro

1 lemon, cut into wedges

1 Preheat the oven to 325°F/160°C. In a heavy-bottom pan, dry-fry the almonds and coconut, then set aside.

2 Heat the oil in a skillet and sauté the onion, stirring, until golden brown.

3 Put the ginger, garlic, chili powder, garam masala, and salt in a bowl and mix in the yogurt. Add the almonds and coconut and mix.

4 Add the onions to the spice mixture and blend, then set aside.

5 Arrange the chicken quarters in the bottom of an ovenproof dish. Spoon the yogurt and spice mixture over the chicken.

6 Cook in the oven for 35–45 minutes, or until the chicken is tender and the juices run clear when a skewer is inserted into the thickest part of the meat. Garnish with cilantro and lemon wedges and serve with a green salad.

COOK'S TIP

If you want a spicier dish, add more chili powder and garam masala.

chicken with pearl onions & green peas

serves four

9 oz/250 g pork fat

salt and pepper

2 oz/55 g butter

16 pearl onions or shallots

2 lb 4 oz/1 kg boneless
   chicken pieces

2 tbsp all-purpose flour

2½ cups chicken stock

1 bouquet garni sachet

1 lb 2 oz/500 g shelled fresh peas

COOK'S TIP

If you want to cut down on the
fat, use lean bacon, cut into
small cubes, rather than pork fat.

---

1 Preheat the oven to 400°F/200°C.
Cut the pork fat into small cubes.
Bring a pan of lightly salted water to
a boil. Add the pork fat cubes and let
simmer for 3 minutes. Drain and dry on
paper towels.

2 Melt the butter in a large skillet.
Add the pork fat and onions or
shallots and sauté gently for 3 minutes,
or until lightly browned.

3 Remove the pork fat and onions
from the skillet and set aside
until required. Add the chicken pieces
to the skillet and cook until browned
all over. Transfer the chicken to a large,
ovenproof casserole.

4 Add the flour to the skillet and
cook, stirring, until it starts to
brown. Slowly blend in the stock.

5 Pour the sauce over the chicken
and add the bouquet garni.
Cover the casserole and cook in the
oven for 35 minutes, or until the
chicken is tender and the juices run
clear when a skewer is inserted into
the thickest part of the meat.

6 Remove and discard the bouquet
garni about 10 minutes before
the end of the cooking time and stir in
the peas and reserved pork fat and
onions. Taste and adjust the seasoning,
if necessary. Return to the oven.

7 To serve, place the chicken pieces
on a large platter, surrounded by
the pork, peas, and onions.

jamaican hotchpotch

serves four

2 tsp corn oil

4 chicken drumsticks

4 chicken thighs

1 onion

1 lb 10 oz/750 g piece pumpkin
    or squash

1 green bell pepper

1-inch/2.5-cm piece fresh
    gingerroot, finely chopped

14 oz/400 g canned
    chopped tomatoes

1¼ cups chicken stock

¼ cup split red lentils, rinsed

garlic salt and cayenne pepper

12 oz/350 g canned corn kernels,
    drained

crusty bread, to serve

VARIATION

If you can't find fresh gingerroot,
add 1 teaspoon of ground
allspice for a fragrant aroma.
If squash or pumpkin is not
available, rutabaga makes a very
good substitute.

1 Preheat the oven to 375°F/190°C. Heat the oil in a large, ovenproof casserole. Add the chicken joints and cook until golden brown, turning frequently.

2 Using a sharp knife, slice the onion, then peel and dice the pumpkin and seed and slice the green bell pepper.

3 Drain any excess fat from the casserole and add the onion, pumpkin, and bell pepper. Gently cook for a few minutes until lightly browned. Add the ginger, tomatoes, stock, and lentils. Season lightly with garlic salt and cayenne pepper.

4 Cover the casserole and cook in the oven for 1 hour, or until the vegetables and chicken are tender and the chicken juices run clear when a skewer is inserted into the thickest part of the meat.

5 Add the corn and cook for an additional 5 minutes. Taste and adjust the seasoning, if necessary, then serve with crusty bread.

rich mediterranean chicken casserole

serves four

8 boneless chicken thighs

2 tbsp olive oil

1 red onion, sliced

2 garlic cloves, crushed

1 large red bell pepper, seeded and
thickly sliced

thinly pared rind and juice of
1 small orange

½ cup chicken stock

14 oz/400 g canned
chopped tomatoes

1 oz/25 g sun-dried tomatoes,
thinly sliced

1 tbsp chopped fresh thyme

generous ¼ cup pitted black olives

salt and pepper

fresh crusty bread, to serve

TO GARNISH

orange rind

fresh thyme sprigs

COOK'S TIP

Sun-dried tomatoes have a dense
texture and concentrated taste,
and add intense flavor to
slow-cooking casseroles.

1 Dry-fry the chicken in a large,
heavy-bottom or nonstick skillet
over fairly high heat, turning
occasionally, until golden brown.
Using a slotted spoon, drain off any
excess fat from the chicken and transfer
to a large, ovenproof casserole.

2 Heat the oil in the skillet. Add
the onion, garlic, and bell pepper
and sauté over medium heat for 3–
4 minutes. Transfer to the casserole.

3 Add the orange rind and juice,
stock, canned tomatoes, and sun-
dried tomatoes and stir to mix.

4 Bring to a boil, then cover the
casserole and let simmer very
gently over low heat for 1 hour, stirring
occasionally, until the chicken is tender.
Add the chopped thyme and black
olives, then season to taste with salt
and pepper.

5 Sprinkle orange rind and thyme
sprigs over the casserole to
garnish, and serve with crusty bread.

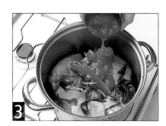

pot roast orange & sesame chicken

serves four

2 tbsp corn oil

1 chicken, weighing 3 lb 5 oz/
   1.5 kg

2 large oranges

2 pearl onions, cut into fourths

1 lb 2 oz/500 g small whole carrots
   or thin carrots, cut into 2-inch/
   5-cm lengths

salt and pepper

⅔ cup orange juice

2 tbsp brandy

2 tbsp sesame seeds

1 tbsp cornstarch

1 tbsp water

VARIATION

Use lemons instead of oranges
for a sharper citrus flavor and
place a fresh thyme sprig in the
chicken cavity with the lemon
half, because they are a good
flavor combination.

1 Preheat the oven to 375°F/190°C. Heat the oil in a large, deep, ovenproof casserole. Add the chicken and cook, turning occasionally, until evenly browned. Remove the chicken.

2 Cut 1 orange in half and place 1 half inside the chicken cavity. Put the chicken back in the casserole and arrange the onions and carrots around it.

3 Season well with salt and pepper and pour over the orange juice.

4 Cut the remaining oranges into thin wedges and tuck around the chicken in the casserole, among the vegetables.

5 Cover and cook in the oven for 1½ hours, or until the vegetables and chicken are tender and the chicken juices run clear when a skewer is inserted into the thickest part of the meat. Uncover and sprinkle with the brandy and sesame seeds, then return to the oven for 10 minutes.

6 To serve, transfer the chicken to a large platter. Place the vegetables around the chicken. Skim any excess fat from the juices in the casserole. Blend the cornstarch with the water, then stir into the juices and bring to a boil, stirring constantly. Season to taste with salt and pepper, then serve the sauce with the chicken.

caribbean chicken

serves four

8 skinless chicken drumsticks

2 limes

1 tsp cayenne pepper

2 ripe mangoes

1 tbsp corn oil

2 tbsp brown sugar

2 tbsp coarsely grated coconut
(optional), for sprinkling

TO GARNISH

lime wedges

cilantro sprigs

COOK'S TIP

When buying mangoes, bear in mind that the skin of ripe mangoes varies in color from green to pinky-red and the flesh from pale yellow to bright orange. Choose mangoes that yield to gentle pressure.

1 Using a sharp knife, slash the chicken drumsticks at intervals, then place them in a large, nonmetallic bowl.

2 Grate the rind from the limes and set aside until required.

3 Squeeze the juice from the limes and sprinkle over the chicken with the cayenne pepper. Cover and let marinate in the refrigerator for at least 2 hours, or preferably overnight.

4 Peel the mangoes. Cut lengthwise either side of the central seed. Discard the seed and slice the flesh.

5 Drain the chicken drumsticks using a slotted spoon and set aside the marinade. Heat the oil in a wide, heavy-bottom skillet. Add the chicken drumsticks and sauté, turning frequently, until golden. Stir in the marinade, reserved lime rind, mango slices, and the sugar.

6 Cover the skillet and let simmer gently, stirring occasionally, for 15 minutes, or until the chicken is tender and the juices run clear when a skewer is inserted into the thickest part of the meat. Sprinkle with grated coconut, if using, and garnish with lime wedges and cilantro sprigs.

Vegetables

Nutritionists tell us that we should eat more vegetables, but it isn't always easy to persuade the family to eat up their greens, especially if they are sitting in an unappetizing heap on the side of the plate. This chapter provides the answer with a spectacular collection of mouthwatering vegetable dishes—soups, bakes, risottos, casseroles, and curries. Beans, peas, lentils, broccoli, cauliflower, mushrooms, bell peppers, onions, zucchini, tomatoes, even the humble potato, all take a starring role and are combined with each other for a melt-in-the-mouth medley or with other ingredients, such as pasta, to satisfy even the hungriest appetite. A vegetarian main course is an easy way to ring the changes in the weekly menu. From Mushroom and Cheese Risotto (see page 171) to Coconut Vegetable Curry (see page 191), vegetables have never looked—or tasted—so good.

roasted mediterranean vegetable soup

serves six

2–3 tbsp olive oil

1 lb 9 oz/700 g ripe tomatoes, peeled, cored, and halved

3 large yellow bell peppers, halved and seeded

3 zucchini, halved lengthwise

1 small eggplant, halved lengthwise

4 garlic cloves, halved

2 onions, cut into eighths

salt and pepper

pinch of dried thyme

4 cups vegetable stock

½ cup light cream

shredded fresh basil leaves, to garnish

1 Preheat the oven to 375°F/190°C. Brush a large, shallow baking dish with oil. Laying cut-side down, arrange the tomatoes, bell peppers, zucchini, and eggplant in 1 layer (use 2 dishes if necessary). Tuck the garlic and onions into the gaps and drizzle the vegetables with the remaining oil. Season lightly with salt and pepper and sprinkle with thyme.

2 Bake the vegetables in the oven, uncovered, for 30–35 minutes, or until soft and browned around the edges. Let cool, then scrape out the eggplant flesh and remove the skin from the bell peppers.

3 Working in batches, put the eggplant and bell pepper flesh, together with the zucchini, into a food processor and chop to the consistency of salsa or pickle; do not purée. Alternatively, place in a bowl and chop with a knife.

4 Combine the stock with the chopped vegetable mixture in a pan and let simmer over medium heat for 20–30 minutes, or until all the vegetables are tender and the flavors have completely blended.

5 Stir in the cream and heat the soup through over low heat for 5 minutes, stirring occasionally. Taste and adjust the seasoning, if necessary. Ladle the soup into warmed bowls and garnish with basil, then serve.

138

tuscan bean & vegetable soup

serves four

1 onion, chopped

1 garlic clove, finely chopped

2 celery stalks, sliced

1 large carrot, diced

14 oz/400 g canned
    chopped tomatoes

⅔ cup Italian dry red wine

5 cups vegetable stock

1 tsp dried oregano

15 oz/425 g canned mixed beans
    and lentils

2 zucchini, diced

1 tbsp tomato paste

salt and pepper

TO SERVE

Pesto (see page 141) or mayonnaise

crusty bread

COOK'S TIP

Use a jar of good quality pesto
from the supermarket as the
garnish if you are too busy to
make your own.

1 Place the onion, garlic, celery, and carrot in a large pan. Stir in the chopped tomatoes, wine, vegetable stock, and oregano.

2 Bring to a boil, then reduce the heat and let simmer, covered, for 15 minutes. Stir the beans and lentils into the mixture with the zucchini, and cook, uncovered, for an additional 5 minutes.

3 Add the tomato paste to the mixture and season to taste with salt and pepper. Heat through, stirring occasionally, for an additional 2–3 minutes, but be careful not to allow the mixture to boil again.

4 Ladle the soup into warmed bowls and serve with a spoonful of Pesto or mayonnaise on each portion, accompanied by chunks of crusty bread.

tuscan onion soup

serves four

1¾ oz/50 g pancetta, diced

1 tbsp olive oil

4 large onions, thinly sliced
into rings

3 garlic cloves, chopped

3½ cups hot chicken or
ham stock

4 slices ciabatta or other
Italian bread

3 heaping tbsp butter

scant ¾ cup coarsely grated Gruyère
or Cheddar cheese

salt and pepper

COOK'S TIP
Pancetta is available from most
delicatessens and some large
supermarkets, but you can use
unsmoked bacon instead.

1 Dry-fry the pancetta in a large pan for 3–4 minutes, or until it starts to brown. Remove the pancetta from the pan and set aside until required.

2 Add the oil to the pan and cook the onions and garlic over high heat for 4 minutes. Reduce the heat, then cover and cook for 15 minutes, or until the onions and garlic are lightly caramelized.

3 Add the stock to the pan and bring to a boil, then reduce the heat and let the mixture simmer, covered, for 10 minutes.

4 Preheat the broiler. Toast the ciabatta under the hot broiler for 2–3 minutes on each side, or until golden. Spread the toasted bread with butter and top each slice with grated cheese. Cut into bite-size pieces.

5 Add the reserved pancetta to the soup and season to taste with salt and pepper. Pour into 4 soup bowls and top with the toasted bread.

green vegetable soup with basil pesto

serves six

1 tbsp olive oil

1 onion, finely chopped

1 large leek, split and thinly sliced

1 celery stalk, thinly sliced

1 carrot, quartered and thinly sliced

1 garlic clove, finely chopped

6 cups water

1 potato, diced

1 parsnip, finely diced

1 small kohlrabi or turnip, diced

5½ oz/150 g green beans, cut into
small pieces

1⅓ cups fresh or frozen peas

2 small zucchini, quartered
and sliced

14 oz/400 g canned flageolets,
rinsed and drained

salt and pepper

generous 2 cups fresh spinach
leaves, finely shredded

PESTO

1 large garlic clove, very
finely chopped

5 tbsp fresh basil leaves

4 tbsp extra virgin olive oil

¾ cup freshly grated
Parmesan cheese

1 Heat the oil in a large pan. Cook the onion and leek over low heat, stirring occasionally, for 5 minutes. Add the celery, carrot, and garlic, then cover and cook for an additional 5 minutes.

2 Add the water, potato, parsnip, kohlrabi, and green beans. Bring to a boil, then reduce the heat and let simmer, covered, for 5 minutes.

3 Add the peas, zucchini, and flageolets and season to taste with salt and pepper. Cover and let simmer for 25 minutes, or until all the vegetables are tender.

4 Meanwhile, make the pesto. Put all the ingredients in a food processor and process until smooth, scraping down the sides as necessary. Alternatively, pound together using a mortar and pestle.

5 Add the spinach to the soup and let simmer for 5 minutes. Stir in a spoonful of the pesto. Ladle the soup into bowls and hand round the remaining pesto separately.

vegetable soup with cannellini beans

serves four

1 small eggplant

2 large tomatoes

1 potato, peeled

1 carrot, peeled

1 leek

14 oz/400 g canned
cannellini beans

3½ cups hot vegetable or
chicken stock

2 tsp dried basil

⅛ cup dried porcini mushrooms,
soaked for 10 minutes in enough
warm water to cover

1¾ oz/50 g dried vermicelli

3 tbsp Pesto (see page 141 or use
store-bought)

freshly grated Parmesan cheese,
to serve (optional)

1 Slice the eggplant into rings
about ½ inch/1 cm thick, then cut
each ring into 4.

2 Cut the tomatoes and potato into
small dice. Cut the carrot into
sticks about 1 inch/2.5 cm long and
slice the leek into rings.

3 Place the beans and their liquid in
a large pan. Add the eggplant,
tomatoes, potato, carrot, and leek,
stirring to mix.

COOK'S TIP

Porcini are a wild mushroom
grown in southern Italy. When
dried and rehydrated, they have
a very intense flavor, so although
they are expensive to buy, only a
small amount is required to add
flavor to soups or risottos.

4 Add the stock to the pan and
bring to a boil. Reduce the heat
and let simmer for 15 minutes.

5 Add the basil, the mushrooms
and their soaking liquid, and the
vermicelli and let simmer for 5 minutes,
or until all the vegetables are tender.

6 Remove the pan from the heat
and stir in the Pesto. Serve the
soup with grated Parmesan cheese,
if wished.

brown lentil soup with pasta

serves four

4 lean bacon slices, cut into
  small squares

1 onion, chopped

2 garlic cloves, crushed

2 celery stalks, chopped

1¾ oz/50 g dried farfalline or
  spaghetti, broken into
  small pieces

14 oz/400 g canned brown
  lentils, drained

5 cups hot ham or
  vegetable stock

2 tbsp chopped fresh mint

1 Place the bacon in a large skillet with the onion, garlic, and celery. Dry-fry for 4–5 minutes, stirring, until the onion is tender and the bacon is just starting to brown.

2 Add the pasta pieces to the skillet and cook, stirring, for 1 minute to coat the pasta in the oil.

COOK'S TIP

If you prefer to use dried lentils, add the stock before the pasta and cook for 1–1¼ hours, or until the lentils are tender. Add the pasta and cook for an additional 12–15 minutes.

VARIATION

Any type of pasta can be used in this recipe—try fusilli, conchiglie, or rigatoni, if you prefer.

3 Add the lentils and the stock and bring to a boil. Reduce the heat and let simmer for 12–15 minutes, or until the pasta is tender.

4 Remove the skillet from the heat and stir in the mint.

5 Transfer the soup to warmed soup bowls and serve at once.

lentil, pasta & vegetable soup

serves four

1 tbsp olive oil

1 onion, chopped

4 garlic cloves, finely chopped

12 oz/350 g carrots, sliced

1 celery stalk, sliced

generous 1 cup split red lentils, washed

2½ cups vegetable stock

3 cups boiling water

salt and pepper

5½ oz/150 g dried pasta

⅔ cup mascarpone, plus extra to serve

2 tbsp chopped fresh parsley, to garnish

COOK'S TIP

Avoid boiling the soup once the mascarpone has been added or it will separate and become watery, spoiling the appearance of the soup.

1 Heat the oil in a large pan over medium heat and sauté the onion, garlic, carrots, and celery, stirring gently, for 5 minutes, or until starting to soften.

2 Add the lentils, stock, and water. Season well with salt and pepper, stir and return to a boil. Reduce the heat and let simmer, uncovered, for 15 minutes, or until the lentils are completely tender. Let cool for 10 minutes.

3 Meanwhile, bring a separate pan of water to a boil and cook the pasta according to the package directions. Drain well and set aside.

4 Transfer the soup to a food processor or blender and process until smooth. Return to a clean pan and add the pasta. Return to a simmer and heat for 2–3 minutes, or until piping hot. Remove from the heat and stir in the mascarpone. Taste and adjust the seasoning if necessary.

5 Serve, garnished with pepper and parsley, with extra mascarpone, if wished.

great northern bean & pasta soup

serves four

1½ cups great Northern beans,
   soaked for 3 hours in cold water
   and drained

4 tbsp olive oil

2 large onions, sliced

3 garlic cloves, chopped

14 oz/400 g canned
   chopped tomatoes

1 tsp dried oregano

1 tsp tomato paste

3½ cups water

scant 1 cup dried fusilli or
   conchigliette

salt and pepper

4 oz/115 g sun-dried tomatoes,
   drained and thinly sliced

1 tbsp chopped fresh cilantro or
   flatleaf parsley

2 tbsp Parmesan cheese shavings,
   to serve

1 Put the beans in a large pan, then add enough cold water to cover and bring to a boil. Boil rapidly over high heat for 15 minutes. Drain the beans and keep warm until required.

2 Heat the oil in a large pan over medium heat and sauté the onions for 2–3 minutes, or until they are just starting to change color. Stir in the garlic and cook for 1 minute. Stir in the canned tomatoes, oregano, and tomato paste.

3 Add the water and the beans to the pan. Bring to a boil, then reduce the heat, and let simmer, covered, for 45 minutes, or until the beans are tender.

COOK'S TIP

If preferred, place the beans in a pan of cold water and bring to a boil. Remove from the heat and let the beans cool in the water. Drain and rinse the beans before using.

4 Add the pasta to the pan and season to taste with salt and pepper. Stir in the sun-dried tomatoes and return to a boil. Reduce the heat, then partially cover and let simmer for 10 minutes, or until the pasta is tender but still firm to the bite.

5 Stir the cilantro into the soup. Ladle into warmed bowls, then sprinkle over the Parmesan cheese and serve at once.

pea & egg noodle soup

serves four

3 rindless smoked bacon
    slices, diced

1 large onion, chopped

1 tbsp butter

1 lb/450 g dried peas, soaked
    in cold water for 2 hours
    and drained

10 cups chicken stock

salt and pepper

8 oz/225 g dried egg noodles

⅔ cup heavy cream

chopped fresh parsley, to garnish

Parmesan cheese croutons (see
    Cook's Tip), to serve

1 Put the bacon, onion, and butter into a large pan and cook over low heat for 6 minutes.

2 Add the peas and the stock to the pan and bring to a boil. Season lightly with salt and pepper. Reduce the heat, then cover and let simmer for 1½ hours.

3 Add the egg noodles to the pan and let simmer for an additional 15 minutes.

4 Pour in the cream and blend thoroughly. Transfer to a warmed tureen and garnish with parsley. Top with the croutons and serve.

COOK'S TIP

To make Parmesan cheese croutons, cut a French stick into slices. Coat lightly with olive oil and sprinkle with Parmesan. Broil for about 30 seconds.

potato, apple & arugula soup

serves four

4 tbsp butter

2 lb/900 g waxy potatoes, diced

1 red onion, cut into fourths

1 tbsp lemon juice

4 cups chicken stock

1 lb/450 g eating apples, peeled
    and diced

pinch of ground allspice

generous 1 cup arugula leaves, plus
    extra to garnish

salt and pepper

warmed crusty bread, to serve

TO GARNISH

slices of red apple

chopped scallions

COOK'S TIP

If arugula is unavailable, use
baby spinach leaves instead for a
similar flavor.

1 Melt the butter in a large pan and add the potatoes and onion. Sauté gently for 5 minutes, stirring constantly.

2 Add the lemon juice, chicken stock, apples, and allspice and stir to combine.

3 Bring to a boil, then reduce the heat to a simmer and cook, covered, for 15 minutes.

4 Add the arugula to the soup and cook for 10 minutes, or until the potatoes are cooked through.

5 Transfer half the soup to a food processor or blender. Process for 1 minute. Stir the purée into the soup in the pan and heat through.

6 Season to taste with salt and pepper. Ladle into warmed soup bowls and garnish with the arugula, apple slices, and scallions. Serve at once with warmed crusty bread.

sweet potato & onion soup

serves four

2 tbsp vegetable oil

2 lb/900 g sweet potatoes, diced

1 carrot, diced

2 onions, sliced

2 garlic cloves, crushed

2½ cups vegetable stock

1¼ cups unsweetened
   orange juice

1 cup lowfat plain yogurt

2 tbsp chopped cilantro

salt and pepper

TO GARNISH

cilantro sprigs

strips of orange rind

1 Heat the oil in a large, heavy-bottom pan and add the sweet potatoes, carrot, onions, and garlic. Sauté the vegetables over low heat, stirring constantly, for 5 minutes, or until softened.

2 Pour in the stock and orange juice and bring to a boil.

3 Reduce the heat, then cover the soup and let simmer for 20 minutes, or until the sweet potatoes and carrot are tender.

4 Transfer the mixture to a food processor or blender in batches and process for 1 minute until smooth. Return the purée to the rinsed-out pan.

COOK'S TIP
This soup can be chilled before serving, if preferred. If chilling, stir the yogurt into the dish just before serving. Serve in chilled bowls.

5 Stir in the yogurt and chopped cilantro and season to taste with salt and pepper.

6 Serve in warmed soup bowls and garnish with cilantro sprigs and orange rind.

corn, potato & cheese soup

serves four

2 tbsp butter

2 shallots, finely chopped

8 oz/225 g potatoes, diced

4 tbsp all-purpose flour

2 tbsp dry white wine

1¼ cups milk

11½ oz/325 g canned corn
    kernels, drained

¾ cup grated Gruyère, Emmental, or
    Cheddar cheese

8–10 fresh sage leaves, chopped

scant 2 cups heavy cream

fresh sage sprigs, to garnish

CROUTONS

2–3 slices day-old white bread

2 tbsp olive oil

1 To make the croutons, cut the crusts off the bread slices, then cut the remaining bread into ¼-inch/ 5-mm squares. Heat the oil in a heavy-bottom skillet and add the bread cubes. Cook, tossing and stirring constantly, until evenly colored. Drain the croutons thoroughly on paper towels and set aside.

2 Melt the butter in a large, heavy-bottom pan. Add the shallots and cook over low heat, stirring occasionally, for 5 minutes, or until softened. Add the potatoes and cook, stirring, for 2 minutes.

3 Sprinkle in the flour and cook, stirring, for 1 minute. Remove the pan from the heat and stir in the wine, then gradually stir in the milk. Return the pan to the heat and bring to a boil, stirring constantly, then reduce the heat and let simmer.

4 Stir in the corn, cheese, sage, and cream and heat through gently until the cheese has just melted. Ladle the soup into warmed bowls, then sprinkle over the croutons and garnish with sage sprigs. Serve at once.

COOK'S TIP

When you are cooking croutons, make sure that the oil is very hot before adding the bread cubes, otherwise the cubes may turn out soggy rather than crisp.

broccoli soup with cream cheese

serves four

14 oz/400 g broccoli
(from 1 large head)

2 tsp butter

1 tsp oil

1 onion, finely chopped

1 leek, thinly sliced

1 small carrot, finely chopped

3 tbsp long-grain rice

3½ cups water

1 bay leaf

salt and pepper

freshly grated nutmeg

4 tbsp heavy cream

scant ½ cup soft cheese

croutons (see Cook's Tip on
page 151), to serve

1 Divide the broccoli into small florets and cut off the stems. Peel the large stems and then chop all the stems into small pieces.

2 Heat the butter and oil in a large pan over medium heat and add the onion, leek, and carrot. Cook the vegetables for 3–4 minutes, stirring frequently, until the onion is softened.

3 Add the broccoli stems, rice, water, bay leaf, and a pinch of salt. Bring just to a boil, then reduce the heat to low. Cover the soup and let simmer for 15 minutes. Add the broccoli florets and cook, covered, for an additional 15–20 minutes, or until the rice and vegetables are tender. Remove and discard the bay leaf.

4 Season the soup with nutmeg and pepper, and more salt, if needed. Stir in the cream and soft cheese. Let simmer over low heat for a few minutes until heated through, stirring occasionally. Adjust the seasoning if necessary. Ladle into warmed bowls and serve sprinkled with the croutons.

spicy zucchini soup with rice & lime

serves four

2 tbsp vegetable oil

4 garlic cloves, thinly sliced

1–2 tbsp mild red chili powder

¼–½ tsp ground cumin

6 cups chicken, vegetable, or
    beef stock

2 zucchini, cut into
    bite-size chunks

4 tbsp long-grain rice

salt and pepper

fresh oregano sprigs, to garnish

lime wedges, to serve

COOK'S TIP

Choose zucchini that are firm to
the touch and have shiny skin.
They should not be too large.

1 Heat the oil in a heavy-bottom pan. Add the garlic and cook for 2 minutes, or until softened and just starting to change color. Add the chili powder and cumin and cook over medium–low heat for 1 minute.

2 Stir in the stock, zucchini, and rice, then cook over medium–high heat for 10 minutes, or until the zucchini are just tender and the rice is cooked through. Season the soup to taste with salt and pepper.

3 Ladle into soup bowls, then garnish with oregano sprigs and serve with lime wedges.

VARIATION

Instead of rice, use rice-shaped
pasta, such as orzo or semone
de melone, or very thin pasta
known as fideo. Use yellow
summer squash instead of the
zucchini and add cooked pinto
beans in place of the rice.
Diced tomatoes also make
a tasty addition.

calabrian mushroom soup

serves four

2 tbsp olive oil

1 onion, chopped

1 lb/450 g mixed mushrooms, such
as cep, oyster, and white

1¼ cups milk

3½ cups hot vegetable stock

salt and pepper

8 slices rustic bread or French stick

3 tbsp butter, melted

2 garlic cloves, crushed

scant ¾ cup finely grated Gruyère
cheese

COOK'S TIP

Mushrooms absorb liquid, which
can lessen the flavor and affect
cooking properties. Wipe them
with a damp cloth rather than
rinsing them in water.

1 Heat the oil in a large skillet and
cook the onion for 3–4 minutes,
or until softened and golden.

2 Wipe each mushroom with
a damp cloth and cut any
large mushrooms into smaller,
bite-size pieces.

3 Add the mushrooms to the skillet,
stirring quickly to coat in the oil.

4 Add the milk to the skillet and
bring to a boil. Reduce the
heat, then cover and let simmer for
5 minutes. Gradually stir in the hot
stock and salt and pepper to taste.

5 Preheat the broiler. Toast the
bread under the hot broiler on
both sides until golden.

VARIATION

Supermarkets stock a wide
variety of wild mushrooms. If you
prefer, use a combination of
cultivated and wild mushrooms.

6 Mix the butter and garlic
together and spoon generously
over the toast.

7 Place the toast in the bottom of a
large tureen or divide it between
4 individual serving bowls and pour
over the hot soup. Top with the grated
cheese and serve at once.

cheese & vegetable chowder

serves four

2 tbsp butter

1 large onion, finely chopped

1 large leek, split lengthwise and
thinly sliced

1–2 garlic cloves, crushed

generous ⅓ cup all-purpose flour

5 cups vegetable stock

3 carrots, finely diced

2 celery stalks, finely diced

1 turnip, finely diced

1 large potato, finely diced

3–4 fresh thyme sprigs or
⅛ tsp dried thyme

1 bay leaf

1½ cups light cream

10½ oz/300 g sharp Cheddar
cheese, grated

salt and pepper

chopped fresh parsley, to garnish

1 Melt the butter in a large, heavy-bottom pan over medium–low heat. Add the onion, leek, and garlic. Cover and cook, stirring frequently, for 5 minutes, or until the vegetables are starting to soften.

2 Stir in the flour and cook for 2 minutes. Add a little of the stock and stir, scraping the bottom of the pan to mix in the flour. Bring to a boil, stirring frequently, and slowly stir in the remaining stock.

3 Add the carrots, celery, turnip, potato, thyme, and bay leaf. Reduce the heat, then cover and let simmer, stirring occasionally, for 35 minutes, or until the vegetables are tender. Remove the bay leaf and thyme sprigs and discard.

4 Stir in the cream and let simmer over very low heat for 5 minutes.

5 Add the cheese a handful at a time, stirring constantly for 1 minute after each addition to make sure it is completely melted. Taste the soup and adjust the seasoning, adding salt if needed and pepper to taste.

6 Ladle the soup into bowls and sprinkle with parsley, then serve.

mexican vegetable soup with tortilla chips

serves four–six

2 tbsp vegetable or virgin olive oil

1 onion, finely chopped

4 garlic cloves, finely chopped

¼– ½ tsp ground cumin

2–3 tsp mild chili powder, such as
    ancho or New Mexico

1 carrot, sliced

1 waxy potato, diced

12 oz/350 g diced fresh or
    canned tomatoes

1 zucchini, diced

¼ small cabbage, shredded

4 cups vegetable or chicken stock
    or water

corn kernels cut from
    1 ear fresh corn or canned

about 10 green or string beans,
    cut into bite-size lengths

salt and pepper

TO SERVE

4–6 tbsp chopped cilantro

salsa of your choice or chopped
    fresh chili, to taste

tortilla chips

1 Heat the oil in a heavy-bottom sauté pan or pan. Add the onion and garlic and cook for a few minutes until softened, then sprinkle in the cumin and chili powder. Stir in the carrot, potato, tomatoes, zucchini, and cabbage and cook for 2 minutes, stirring the mixture occasionally.

2 Pour in the stock or water. Cover and cook over medium heat for 20 minutes, or until the vegetables are tender.

3 Add extra stock or water if necessary, then stir in the corn and beans and cook for an additional 5–10 minutes, or until the beans are tender. Season to taste with salt and pepper, bearing in mind that the tortilla chips may be salty.

4 Ladle the soup into soup bowls and sprinkle each portion with chopped cilantro. Top with a little salsa or chili, then add a handful of tortilla chips.

mexican tomato rice

serves six–eight

2 cups long-grain rice

1 large onion, chopped

2–3 garlic cloves, crushed

12 oz/350 g canned Italian
plum tomatoes

3–4 tbsp olive oil

4 cups chicken stock

1 tbsp tomato paste

1 fresh habanero or other hot chili

salt and pepper

1½ cups frozen peas, thawed

4 tbsp chopped cilantro,
plus extra to serve

TO SERVE

1 large avocado, peeled, pitted,
sliced, and sprinkled with
lime juice

lime wedges

4 scallions, chopped

1 In a bowl, cover the rice with hot water and set aside to stand for 15 minutes. Drain, then rinse under cold running water and drain again.

2 Place the onion and garlic in a food processor and process until a smooth purée forms. Scrape the purée into a small bowl and set aside. Put the tomatoes in the food processor and process until smooth, then press through a nylon strainer into another bowl, pushing through any solids with the back of a wooden spoon.

3 Heat the oil in an ovenproof casserole over medium heat. Add the rice and cook, stirring frequently, for 4 minutes until golden and translucent. Add the onion purée and cook, stirring frequently, for an additional 2 minutes. Add the stock, processed tomatoes, and tomato paste and bring to a boil.

4 Using a pin or long needle, carefully pierce the chili in 2–3 places. Add to the rice and season to taste with salt and pepper, then reduce the heat to low. Cover and let simmer for 25 minutes, or until the rice is tender and the liquid is just absorbed. Discard the chili, then stir in the peas and cilantro and cook for an additional 5 minutes to heat through.

5 To serve, gently fork the rice mixture into a warmed large, shallow serving bowl. Arrange the avocado slices and lime wedges on top. Sprinkle over the scallions and some chopped cilantro and serve at once.

baked tomato rice

serves four

2 tbsp vegetable oil

1 onion, coarsely chopped

1 red bell pepper, seeded
and chopped

2 garlic cloves, finely chopped

½ tsp dried thyme

1½ cups long-grain rice

4 cups chicken or
vegetable stock

8 oz/225 g canned
chopped tomatoes

1 bay leaf

2 tbsp shredded fresh basil

1½ cups grated sharp Cheddar
cheese

2 tbsp snipped fresh chives

4 herbed pork sausages, cooked
and cut into ½-inch/1-cm pieces

2–3 tbsp freshly grated
Parmesan cheese

1 Preheat the oven to 350°F/
180°C. Heat the oil in a large,
ovenproof casserole over medium heat.
Add the onion and bell pepper and
cook, stirring frequently, for 5 minutes,
or until soft and lightly colored. Stir in
the garlic and thyme and cook for an
additional minute.

2 Add the rice and cook, stirring
frequently, for 2 minutes, or until
the rice is well coated and translucent.
Stir in the stock, tomatoes, and bay
leaf. Bring to a boil, then let simmer
rapidly for 5 minutes, or until the stock
is almost completely absorbed.

3 Stir in the basil, Cheddar cheese,
chives, and sausages and bake,
covered, in the oven for 25 minutes.

4 Sprinkle with the Parmesan
cheese and return to the oven,
uncovered, for 5 minutes, or until the
top is golden. Serve hot.

COOK'S TIP

For a vegetarian version, replace
the pork sausages with 14 oz/
400 g canned drained lima
beans, kidney beans, or corn
kernels. Alternatively, try a
mixture of sautéed mushrooms
and zucchini.

milanese sun-dried tomato risotto

serves four

1 tbsp olive oil

2 tbsp butter

1 large onion, finely chopped

generous 1½ cups risotto rice

about 15 saffron threads

⅔ cup white wine

3½ cups hot vegetable or
  chicken stock

8 sun-dried tomatoes, cut into strips

scant 1 cup frozen peas, thawed

1¾ oz/50 g prosciutto, shredded

scant ¾ cup freshly grated Parmesan
  cheese, plus extra for sprinkling

1 Heat the oil and butter in a large skillet. Add the chopped onion and cook for 4–5 minutes, or until softened.

2 Add the rice and saffron to the skillet, stirring well to coat the rice in the oil, and cook for 1 minute.

3 Add the wine and stock slowly to the rice mixture in the skillet, a ladleful at a time, stirring and making sure that all the liquid is absorbed before adding the next ladleful of liquid.

4 About halfway through adding the stock, stir in the tomatoes.

5 When all the wine and stock is incorporated, the rice should be cooked. Test by tasting a grain—if it is still crunchy, add a little more stock and continue cooking. It should take at least 15 minutes to cook.

6 Stir in the peas, prosciutto, and Parmesan cheese. Cook, stirring, for 2–3 minutes, or until hot. Serve with extra Parmesan for sprinkling.

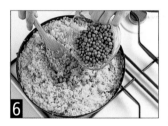

COOK'S TIP

Italian rice is a round, short-grained variety with a nutty flavor, which is essential for a good risotto. Arborio is the very best variety to use.

easy cheese risotto

serves four

4–6 tbsp unsalted butter

1 onion, finely chopped

scant 1½ cups risotto rice

½ cup dry white vermouth or
white wine

5 cups chicken or vegetable
stock, simmering

¾ cup freshly grated Parmesan
cheese, plus extra for sprinkling

salt and pepper

1 Heat about 2 tablespoons of the butter in a large, heavy-bottom pan over medium heat. Add the onion and cook for 2 minutes, or until just starting to soften. Add the rice and cook, stirring, for 2 minutes, or until translucent and well coated with the butter.

2 Pour in the vermouth; it will bubble and steam rapidly and evaporate almost immediately. Add a ladleful (about 1 cup) of the simmering stock and cook, stirring constantly, until the stock is completely absorbed.

3 Continue adding the stock, about half a ladleful at a time, letting each addition be absorbed before adding the next—never let the rice cook "dry". This should take 20–25 minutes. The risotto should have a creamy consistency and the rice should be tender but still firm to the bite.

4 Switch off the heat and stir in the remaining butter and Parmesan cheese. Season to taste with salt and pepper. Cover and let stand for 1 minute, then serve with extra Parmesan cheese for sprinkling.

COOK'S TIP

If you prefer not to use butter,
soften the onion in
2 tablespoons of olive oil and
stir in about 2 tablespoons of
extra virgin olive oil with the
Parmesan at the end.

minted green risotto

serves six

2 tbsp unsalted butter

1 lb/450 g fresh shelled peas or
    thawed frozen peas

2 lb 4 oz/1 kg young spinach leaves

1 bunch fresh mint, leaves stripped
    from stalks

2 tbsp chopped fresh basil

2 tbsp chopped fresh oregano

pinch of freshly grated nutmeg

4 tbsp mascarpone cheese or
    heavy cream

2 tbsp vegetable oil

1 onion, finely chopped

4 celery stems, including leaves,
    finely chopped

2 garlic cloves, finely chopped

½ tsp dried thyme

scant 1½ cups risotto rice

¼ cup dry white vermouth

4 cups chicken or vegetable
    stock, simmering

¾ cup freshly grated
    Parmesan cheese

scallion tassels, to garnish

1 Heat half the butter in a deep skillet over medium–high heat. Add the peas, spinach, herbs, and nutmeg. Cook, stirring, for 3 minutes, or until the spinach is wilted.

2 Transfer to a food processor and process for 15 seconds. Add the mascarpone and process again for 1 minute. Set aside.

3 Heat the oil and remaining butter in a large, heavy-bottom pan over medium heat. Add the onion, celery, garlic, and thyme and cook for 2 minutes, or until softened. Add the rice and cook, stirring, for 2 minutes, or until translucent and well coated.

4 Pour in the vermouth; it will bubble and steam rapidly. When it is almost absorbed, add a ladleful (about 1 cup) of the simmering stock. Cook, stirring constantly, until the stock is completely absorbed.

5 Continue adding the stock, about half a ladleful at a time, letting each addition be absorbed before adding the next. This should take 20–25 minutes. The risotto should have a creamy consistency and the rice should be tender but still firm to the bite. Stir in the spinach-cream mixture and the Parmesan cheese. Serve the risotto at once, garnished with scallion tassels.

wild mushroom risotto

serves six

½ cup dried porcini or
  morel mushrooms
about 1 lb 2 oz/500 g mixed fresh
  wild mushrooms, such as porcini,
  girolles, horse mushrooms, and
  chanterelles, halved if large
4 tbsp olive oil
3–4 garlic cloves, finely chopped
4 tbsp unsalted butter
1 onion, finely chopped
generous 1½ cups risotto rice
¼ cup dry white vermouth
5 cups chicken or vegetable stock,
  simmering
salt and pepper
1 cup freshly grated
  Parmesan cheese
4 tbsp chopped fresh
  flatleaf parsley
6 fresh parsley sprigs, to garnish
crusty bread, to serve

1 Place the dried mushrooms in a heatproof bowl and pour over enough boiling water to cover. Let soak for 30 minutes, then carefully lift out and pat dry. Strain the soaking liquid through a strainer lined with paper towels and set aside.

2 Trim the wild mushrooms and gently brush clean.

3 Heat 3 tablespoons of the oil in a skillet over low heat. Add the fresh mushrooms and sauté for 1–2 minutes. Add the garlic and soaked mushrooms and cook, stirring frequently, for 2 minutes. Transfer to a plate and set aside.

4 Heat the remaining oil and half the butter in a large pan over low heat. Add the onion and cook, stirring occasionally, for 2 minutes, or until softened. Add the rice and cook, stirring, for 2 minutes, or until translucent and well coated. Add the vermouth. When almost absorbed, add a ladleful (about 1 cup) of the stock. Cook, stirring, until the stock is completely absorbed.

5 Continue adding the stock, about half a ladleful at a time, letting each addition be absorbed before adding the next. This should take 20–25 minutes. The risotto should have a creamy consistency and the rice should be tender but still firm to the bite.

6 Add half the reserved mushroom soaking liquid to the risotto and stir in the mushrooms. Season to taste with salt and pepper and add more mushroom liquid, if necessary. Remove from the heat and stir in the remaining butter, the Parmesan cheese, and chopped parsley. Transfer to 6 warmed serving dishes. Garnish with parsley sprigs and serve with crusty bread.

hot pink risotto

serves four–six

generous 1 cup dried sour cherries
    or dried cranberries

1 cup fruity red wine, such as
    Valpolicella

3 tbsp olive oil

1 large red onion, finely chopped

2 celery stalks, finely chopped

½ tsp dried thyme

1 garlic clove, finely chopped

generous 1½ cups risotto rice

5 cups chicken or vegetable stock,
    simmering

4 cooked fresh beet (not pickled),
    diced

2 tbsp chopped fresh dill

2 tbsp snipped fresh chives

salt and pepper

½ cup freshly grated Parmesan
    cheese, to serve (optional)

1 Put the dried cherries in a pan
with the wine and bring to a boil.
Reduce the heat and let simmer for
2–3 minutes, or until slightly reduced.
Remove from the heat and set aside.

2 Heat the oil in a large, heavy-
bottom pan over medium heat.
Add the onion, celery, and thyme and
cook, stirring occasionally, for
2 minutes, or until just starting to
soften. Add the garlic and rice and
cook, stirring, for 2 minutes, or until
the rice is translucent and well coated.

3 Add a ladleful (about 1 cup)
of the simmering stock; it will
bubble and steam rapidly. Cook,
stirring constantly, until the stock is
completely absorbed.

4 Continue adding the stock, about
half a ladleful at a time, letting
each addition be absorbed before
adding the next. This should take
20–25 minutes. The risotto should
have a creamy consistency and the rice
should be tender but still firm to the
bite. Halfway through the cooking
time, remove the cherries from the
wine with a slotted spoon and add to
the risotto with the beet and half the
wine. Continue adding the stock and
remaining wine.

5 Stir in the dill and chives and
season to taste with salt and
pepper. Serve with Parmesan cheese,
if wished.

arugula & tomato risotto

serves four–six

2 tbsp olive oil

2 tbsp unsalted butter

1 large onion, finely chopped

2 garlic cloves, finely chopped

generous 1½ cups risotto rice

½ cup dry white vermouth

6 cups chicken or vegetable stock,
  simmering

6 vine-ripened or Italian
  plum tomatoes, seeded
  and chopped

scant 3 cups wild arugula

handful of fresh basil leaves

1 cup freshly grated
  Parmesan cheese

8 oz/225 g fresh Italian buffalo
  mozzarella, coarsely grated
  or diced

salt and pepper

1 Heat the oil and half the butter in a large skillet. Add the onion and cook for 2 minutes, or until just starting to soften. Stir in the garlic and rice and cook, stirring, for 2 minutes, or until the rice is translucent and well coated.

2 Pour in the vermouth; it will bubble and steam rapidly and evaporate almost immediately. Add a ladleful (about 1 cup) of the stock and cook, stirring, until absorbed.

3 Continue adding the stock, about half a ladleful at a time, letting each addition be absorbed before adding the next. Just before the rice is tender, stir in the tomatoes and arugula. Shred the basil leaves and immediately stir into the risotto. Continue to cook, adding more stock, until the risotto is creamy and the rice is tender but still firm to the bite.

4 Remove from the heat and stir in the remaining butter and cheeses. Season to taste with salt and pepper. Cover and let stand for 1 minute. Serve at once, before the mozzarella melts completely.

roasted pumpkin risotto

serves six

4 tbsp olive oil

4 tbsp unsalted butter, cut into
small pieces

1 lb/450 g pumpkin flesh, cut into
½-inch/1-cm dice

¾ tsp dried sage

2 garlic cloves, finely chopped

salt and pepper

2 tbsp lemon juice

2 large shallots, finely chopped

generous 1½ cups risotto rice

¼ cup dry white vermouth

5 cups chicken stock, simmering

generous ½ cup freshly grated
Parmesan cheese

10½ oz/300 g Gorgonzola cheese,
cut into small pieces

celery leaves, to garnish

1 Preheat the oven to
400°F/200°C. Put half the oil
and about 1 tablespoon of the butter
in a roasting pan and heat in
the oven.

2 Add the pumpkin to the pan and
sprinkle with the sage, half the
garlic, and salt and pepper to taste.
Toss together and roast for 10 minutes,
or until just softened and starting to
caramelize. Transfer to a plate.

3 Coarsely mash about half the
cooked pumpkin with the lemon
juice and reserve with the remaining
diced pumpkin.

4 Heat the remaining oil and
1 tablespoon of the remaining
butter in a large, heavy-bottom pan
over medium heat. Stir in the shallots
and remaining garlic and cook for
1 minute. Add the rice and cook,
stirring, for 2 minutes, or until
translucent and well coated.

5 Pour in the vermouth; it will
bubble and steam rapidly and
evaporate almost immediately. Add
a ladleful (about 1 cup) of the
simmering stock and cook, stirring
constantly, until absorbed.

6 Continue adding the stock, about
half a ladleful at a time, letting
each addition be absorbed before
adding the next. This should take
20–25 minutes. The finished risotto
should have a creamy consistency and
the rice should be tender but still firm
to the bite.

7 Stir the pumpkin into the risotto
with the remaining butter and the
Parmesan cheese. Remove from the
heat and fold in the Gorgonzola. Serve
at once, garnished with celery leaves.

orange-scented risotto

serves four

2 tbsp pine nuts

4 tbsp unsalted butter

2 shallots, finely chopped

1 leek, finely shredded

scant 2 cups risotto rice

2 tbsp orange-flavored liqueur or
dry white vermouth

6 cups chicken or vegetable
stock, simmering

grated rind of 1 orange

juice of 2 oranges, strained

3 tbsp snipped fresh chives

salt and pepper

1 Toast the pine nuts in a skillet over medium heat, stirring and shaking frequently, for 3 minutes, or until golden brown. Set aside.

2 Heat half the butter in a large, heavy-bottom pan over medium heat. Add the shallots and leek and cook for 2 minutes, or until starting to soften. Add the rice and cook, stirring, for 2 minutes, or until translucent and well coated.

3 Pour in the liqueur or vermouth; it will bubble and steam rapidly and evaporate almost immediately. Add a ladleful (about 1 cup) of the stock and cook, stirring, until absorbed. Continue adding the stock, about half a ladleful at a time, letting each addition be absorbed before adding the next— never allow the rice to cook "dry."

4 After about 15 minutes, add the orange rind and juice and continue to cook, adding more stock, until the rice is tender but still firm to the bite. The risotto should have a creamy consistency.

5 Remove from the heat and stir in the remaining butter and 2 tablespoons of the chives. Season to taste with salt and pepper. Spoon into warmed serving dishes and sprinkle with the toasted pine nuts and the remaining chives.

mushroom & cheese risotto

serves four

2 tbsp olive or vegetable oil

generous 1 cup risotto rice

2 garlic cloves, crushed

1 onion, chopped

2 celery stalks, chopped

1 red or green bell pepper, seeded
and chopped

8 oz/225 g mushrooms, sliced

1 tbsp chopped fresh oregano or
1 tsp dried oregano

4 cups vegetable stock

2 oz/55 g sun-dried tomatoes in
olive oil, drained and chopped
(optional)

salt and pepper

½ cup finely grated Parmesan
cheese

TO GARNISH

fresh flatleaf parsley sprigs

fresh bay leaves

1 Heat the oil in a preheated wok
or large skillet. Add the rice and
cook, stirring constantly, for 5 minutes.

2 Add the garlic, onion, celery, and
bell pepper and cook, stirring
constantly, for 5 minutes. Add the
mushrooms and cook for 3–4 minutes.

3 Stir in the oregano and stock.
Heat until just boiling, then
reduce the heat and let simmer,
covered, for 20 minutes, or until
the rice is tender and creamy.

4 Add the sun-dried tomatoes,
if using, and season to taste
with salt and pepper. Stir in half the
Parmesan cheese. Top with the
remaining Parmesan and garnish with
the parsley sprigs and bay leaves,
then serve at once.

171

vegetable jambalaya

serves four

scant ½ cup brown rice

2 tbsp olive oil

2 garlic cloves, crushed

1 red onion, cut into 8 wedges

1 eggplant, diced

1 green bell pepper, diced

1¾ oz/50 g baby corn,
    halved lengthwise

scant ½ cup frozen peas

3½ oz/100 g small broccoli florets

⅔ cup vegetable stock

8 oz/225 g canned
    chopped tomatoes

1 tbsp tomato paste

1 tsp creole seasoning

½ tsp dried red pepper flakes

salt and pepper

1 Cook the rice in a large pan of boiling water for 20 minutes, or until cooked through. Drain and set aside until required.

2 Heat the oil in a heavy-bottom skillet. Add the garlic and onion and cook, stirring constantly, for 2–3 minutes.

3 Add the eggplant, bell pepper, baby corn, peas, and broccoli to the skillet and cook, stirring occasionally, for 2–3 minutes.

COOK'S TIP
Use a mixture of rice,
such as wild or red rice,
for color and texture.

4 Stir in the stock, tomatoes, tomato paste, creole seasoning, and red pepper flakes. Season to taste with salt and pepper and cook over low heat for 15–20 minutes, or until the vegetables are tender.

5 Add the rice to the vegetable mixture and heat through, gently stirring, for 3–4 minutes, or until piping hot. Transfer to warmed serving dishes and serve at once.

fried rice with spicy beans

serves four

3 tbsp corn oil

1 onion, finely chopped

generous 1 cup long-grain rice

1 green bell pepper, diced

1 tsp chili powder

2½ cups boiling water

3½ oz/100 g canned corn
    kernels, drained

8 oz/225 g canned red kidney
    beans, rinsed and drained

2 tbsp chopped fresh cilantro, plus
    extra to garnish (optional)

1 Heat a large wok over medium heat. Add the oil and heat.

2 Add the onion and stir-fry for 2 minutes, or until softened.

3 Reduce the heat, then add the rice, bell pepper, and chili powder and stir-fry for 1 minute.

4 Pour in the boiling water. Return to a boil, then reduce the heat and let simmer for 15 minutes.

5 Stir in the corn, beans, and cilantro and heat through, stirring occasionally.

6 Transfer to a warmed serving bowl and serve hot, sprinkled with extra cilantro, if wished.

COOK'S TIP

For perfect fried rice, the raw rice should ideally be soaked in a bowl of water for a short time before cooking, to remove excess starch. Short-grain Asian rice can be substituted for the long-grain rice.

cashew paella

serves four

2 tbsp olive oil

1 tbsp butter

1 red onion, chopped

scant ¾ cup risotto rice

1 tsp ground turmeric

1 tsp ground cumin

½ tsp chili powder

3 garlic cloves, crushed

1 fresh green chili, sliced

1 green bell pepper, diced

1 red bell pepper, diced

2¾ oz/75 g baby corn,
    halved lengthwise

2 tbsp pitted black olives

1 large tomato, seeded and diced

2 cups vegetable stock

½ cup unsalted cashews

¼ cup frozen peas

salt and pepper

2 tbsp chopped fresh parsley

pinch of cayenne pepper

fresh herbs, to garnish

1 Heat the oil and butter in a large skillet or paella pan until the butter has melted.

2 Add the chopped onion and sauté for 2–3 minutes, stirring constantly, until softened.

3 Stir in the rice, turmeric, cumin, chili powder, garlic, chili, bell peppers, baby corn, olives, and tomato and cook over medium heat for 1–2 minutes, stirring occasionally.

4 Pour in the stock and bring the mixture to a boil. Reduce the heat and cook for 20 minutes, stirring frequently.

5 Add the cashews and peas and cook for an additional 5 minutes, stirring occasionally. Season to taste with salt and pepper and sprinkle with parsley and cayenne pepper. Transfer to warmed serving plates and garnish with fresh herbs. Serve at once.

brown rice, vegetable & herb gratin

serves four

½ cup brown rice

salt and pepper

2 tbsp butter or margarine, plus
    extra for greasing

1 red onion, chopped

2 garlic cloves, crushed

1 carrot, cut into matchsticks

1 zucchini, sliced

2¾ oz/75 g baby corn,
    halved lengthwise

2 tbsp sunflower seeds

3 tbsp chopped fresh mixed herbs

3½ oz/100 g grated
    mozzarella cheese

2 tbsp fresh whole-wheat
    bread crumbs

VARIATION

Use an alternative rice, such as
basmati, and flavor the dish with
curry spices, if you prefer.

1 Preheat the oven to 350°F/
180°C. Lightly grease a
3½-cup ovenproof dish.

2 Cook the rice in a large pan of
lightly salted boiling water for
20 minutes. Drain well.

3 Heat the butter in a skillet.
Add the onion and cook, stirring
constantly, for 2 minutes, or until
softened.

4 Add the garlic, carrot, zucchini,
and baby corn and cook for an
additional 5 minutes, stirring.

5 Mix the rice with the sunflower
seeds and mixed herbs in a bowl
and stir into the skillet.

6 Stir in half the cheese and season
to taste with salt and pepper.

7 Spoon the mixture into the
prepared dish and top with the
bread crumbs and remaining cheese.
Cook in the oven for 25–30 minutes,
or until the cheese starts to turn
golden. Serve at once.

vegetable chili

serves four

1 eggplant, peeled (optional) and
    cut into 1-inch/2.5-cm slices

1 tbsp olive oil, plus extra
    for brushing

1 large red or yellow onion,
    finely chopped

2 red or yellow bell peppers, seeded
    and finely chopped

3–4 garlic cloves, finely chopped
    or crushed

1 lb 12 oz/800 g canned
    chopped tomatoes

1 tbsp mild chili powder

½ tsp ground cumin

½ tsp dried oregano

salt and pepper

2 small zucchini, cut into fourths
    lengthwise and sliced

14 oz/400 g canned kidney beans,
    rinsed and drained

2 cups water

1 tbsp tomato paste

TO GARNISH

6 scallions, finely chopped

1 cup grated Cheddar cheese

1 Brush the eggplant slices on one side with oil. Heat half the oil in a large, heavy-bottom skillet over medium–high heat. Add the eggplant slices, oiled-side up, and cook for 5–6 minutes, or until browned underneath. Turn over and brown the other side. Remove and cut into bite-size pieces.

2 Heat the remaining oil in a large pan over medium heat. Add the onion and bell peppers and cook, stirring occasionally, for 3–4 minutes, or until the onion is just softened but not browned. Add the garlic and cook for an additional 2–3 minutes, or until the onion is just starting to color.

3 Add the tomatoes, chili powder, cumin, and oregano. Season to taste with salt and pepper. Bring just to a boil, then reduce the heat and let simmer gently, covered, for 15 minutes.

4 Add the zucchini, eggplant pieces, and beans. Stir in the water and the tomato paste. Return to a boil, then reduce the heat and let simmer, covered, for 45 minutes, or until the vegetables are tender. Taste the chili and adjust the seasoning if necessary. If you prefer a hotter dish, stir in a little more chili powder.

5 Ladle into warmed bowls and top with scallions and cheese, then serve.

spicy fragrant black bean chili

serves four

2⅓ cups dried black beans

2 tbsp olive oil

1 onion, chopped

5 garlic cloves, coarsely chopped

½–1 tsp ground cumin

½–1 tsp mild red chili powder

1 red bell pepper, seeded and diced

1 carrot, diced

14 oz/400 g fresh tomatoes, diced,
  or chopped canned

1 bunch cilantro, coarsely chopped

salt and pepper

COOK'S TIP

You can use canned beans,
if wished—drain and use
1 cup water in place of the
reserved bean cooking liquid.

1 Soak the beans overnight, then drain. Place in a pan, then cover with water and bring to a boil. Boil for 10 minutes, then reduce the heat and let simmer for 1½ hours, or until tender. Drain well, reserving 1 cup of the cooking liquid.

2 Heat the oil in a skillet. Add the onion and garlic and cook for 2 minutes, until the onion is softened.

3 Stir in the cumin and chili powder and cook for a few seconds. Add the bell pepper, carrot, and tomatoes. Cook over medium heat for 5 minutes.

4 Add half the cilantro and the beans and their reserved liquid. Season to taste with salt and pepper. Let simmer for 30–45 minutes, or until very flavorful and thickened.

5 Stir in the remaining cilantro and adjust the seasoning, then serve at once.

brown rice with fruit & nuts

serves four–six

4 tbsp vegetable ghee or oil

1 large onion, chopped

2 garlic cloves, crushed

1-inch/2.5-cm piece fresh
    gingerroot, finely chopped

1 tsp chili powder

1 tsp cumin seeds

1 tbsp mild or medium curry
    powder or paste

scant 1½ cups brown rice

3½ cups boiling
    vegetable stock

14 oz/400 g canned
    chopped tomatoes

salt and pepper

1 cup no-soak dried apricots or
    peaches, cut into slivers

1 red bell pepper, seeded and diced

¾ cup frozen peas

1–2 small, slightly green bananas

⅓–½ cup toasted mixed nuts

1 Heat the ghee in a large skillet over medium heat, add the onion and sauté for 3 minutes.

2 Stir in the garlic, ginger, chili powder, cumin seeds, curry powder, and rice. Cook gently for 2 minutes, stirring constantly, until the rice is coated in the spiced oil.

3 Pour in the boiling stock, stirring to mix. Add the tomatoes and season to taste with salt and pepper. Bring the mixture to a boil, then reduce the heat and let simmer gently, covered, for 40 minutes, or until the rice is almost cooked and most of the liquid is absorbed.

4 Add the apricots, bell pepper, and peas, then cover and cook for an additional 10 minutes.

5 Remove the skillet from the heat and let stand, covered, for 5 minutes.

6 Peel and slice the bananas. Uncover the rice mixture and toss with a fork to mix. Add the toasted nuts and sliced banana and toss lightly.

7 Transfer the brown rice, fruit, and nuts to a warmed serving dish and serve hot.

asian-style millet pilaf

serves four

scant 2 cups millet grains

1 tbsp vegetable oil

1 bunch scallions, chopped

1 garlic clove, crushed

1 tsp grated fresh gingerroot

1 orange bell pepper, seeded
and diced

2½ cups water

1 orange

salt and pepper

scant ⅔ cup chopped pitted dates

2 tsp sesame oil

scant ¾ cup roasted cashews

2 tbsp pumpkin seeds

Asian salad vegetables, to serve

1 Place the millet in a large pan and toast over medium heat, shaking the pan occasionally, for 4–5 minutes, or until the grains start to crack and pop.

2 Heat the vegetable oil in a separate pan. Add the scallions, garlic, ginger, and bell pepper and cook over medium heat, stirring frequently, for 2–3 minutes, or until just softened but not browned. Add the millet and pour in the water.

3 Using a vegetable peeler, pare the rind from the orange and add to the pan. Squeeze the juice from the orange into the pan. Season to taste with salt and pepper.

4 Bring to a boil, then reduce the heat and cook gently, covered, for 20 minutes, or until all the liquid has been absorbed. Remove the pan from the heat and stir in the dates and sesame oil, then let stand for 10 minutes.

5 Remove and discard the orange rind and stir in the nuts. Pile into a warmed serving dish and sprinkle with pumpkin seeds, then serve at once with Asian salad vegetables.

vegetable curry

serves four

8 oz/225 g turnips or rutabaga

1 eggplant

12 oz/350 g new potatoes

8 oz/225 g cauliflower

8 oz/225 g white mushrooms

1 large onion

8 oz/225 g carrots

6 tbsp vegetable ghee or oil

2 garlic cloves, crushed

2-inch/5-cm piece fresh gingerroot, finely chopped

1–2 fresh green chilies, seeded and chopped

1 tbsp paprika

2 tsp ground coriander

1 tbsp mild or medium curry powder or paste

2 cups vegetable stock

14 oz/400 g canned chopped tomatoes

salt

1 green bell pepper, seeded and sliced

1 tbsp cornstarch

⅔ cup coconut milk

2–3 tbsp ground almonds

cilantro sprigs, to garnish

1 Cut the turnips, eggplant, and potatoes into ½-inch/1-cm cubes. Divide the cauliflower into small florets. Leave the mushrooms whole, or thickly slice if preferred. Slice the onion and carrots.

2 Heat the ghee in a large pan over medium heat, then add the onion, carrots, turnips, potato, and cauliflower and cook for 3 minutes, stirring frequently. Add the garlic, ginger, chilies, paprika, ground coriander, and curry powder and cook for 1 minute, stirring.

3 Add the stock, tomatoes, eggplant, and mushrooms and season to taste with salt. Cover and let simmer gently, stirring occasionally, for 30 minutes, or until tender. Add the bell pepper, then cover and cook for an additional 5 minutes.

4 Blend the cornstarch with the coconut milk and stir into the mixture. Add the almonds and let simmer for 2 minutes, stirring. Taste and adjust the seasoning if necessary. Transfer to serving plates and serve hot, garnished with cilantro sprigs.

green bean & potato curry

serves four

1¼ cups oil

1 tsp cumin seeds

1 tsp mixed mustard and
   onion seeds

4 dried red chilies

3 tomatoes, sliced

1 tsp salt

1 tsp finely chopped fresh
   gingerroot

1 garlic clove, crushed

1 tsp chili powder

7 oz/200 g green beans, sliced

2 potatoes, peeled and diced

1¼ cups water

TO GARNISH

chopped cilantro

2 fresh green chilies, finely chopped

COOK'S TIP

Mustard seeds are often cooked
in oil or ghee (cooking fat similar
to clarified butter) to bring out
their flavor before being
combined with other ingredients.

---

1 Heat the oil in a large, heavy-bottom pan.

2 Add the cumin, mustard and onion seeds, and dried chilies to the pan, stirring well.

3 Add the tomatoes to the pan and stir-fry the mixture for 3–5 minutes.

4 Mix together the salt, ginger, garlic, and chili powder and spoon into the pan. Blend the whole mixture together.

5 Add the beans and potatoes to the pan and stir-fry for 5 minutes.

6 Add the water, then reduce the heat and let simmer for 10–15 minutes, stirring occasionally.

7 Garnish the curry with cilantro and fresh chilies and serve hot.

red curry with cashews

serves four

generous 1 cup coconut milk

1 kaffir lime leaf

¼ tsp light soy sauce

4 baby corn, halved lengthwise

4 oz/115 g broccoli florets

4 oz/115 g green beans, cut
    into pieces

4 tbsp unsalted cashews

15 fresh basil leaves

1 tbsp chopped cilantro

1 tbsp chopped roasted peanuts,
    to garnish

RED CURRY PASTE

7 fresh red chilies, seeded
    and blanched

2 tsp cumin seeds

2 tsp coriander seeds

1-inch/2.5-cm piece fresh gingerroot
    or galangal, chopped

½ lemongrass stem, chopped

1 tsp salt

grated rind of 1 lime

4 garlic cloves, chopped

3 shallots, chopped

2 kaffir lime leaves, shredded

1 tbsp vegetable oil

1 To make the curry paste, grind all the ingredients in a large mortar with a pestle or in a spice grinder. Alternatively, process briefly in a food processor. (The quantity of red curry paste is more than is required for this recipe. Store for up to 3 weeks in a sealed jar in the refrigerator.)

2 Heat a wok or large, heavy-bottom skillet over high heat, then add 3 tablespoons of the red curry paste and stir until it gives off its aroma. Reduce the heat to medium.

3 Add the coconut milk, lime leaf, soy sauce, baby corns, broccoli, beans, and cashews. Bring to a boil, then reduce the heat and let simmer for 10 minutes, or until the vegetables are cooked but still crunchy.

4 Remove and discard the lime leaf and stir in the basil leaves and cilantro. Transfer to a warmed serving dish and garnish with peanuts, then serve at once.

potato & spinach yellow curry

serves four

2 garlic cloves, finely chopped

1¼-inch/3-cm piece fresh gingerroot
    or galangal, finely chopped

1 lemongrass stem, finely chopped

1 tsp coriander seeds

3 tbsp vegetable oil

2 tsp Thai red curry paste

½ tsp ground turmeric

scant 1 cup coconut milk

9 oz/250 g potatoes, cut into
    ¾ -inch/2-cm cubes

generous ⅓ cup vegetable stock

generous 4⅓ cups young spinach
    leaves

1 small onion, thinly sliced
    into rings

COOK'S TIP

Choose a firm, waxy potato for
this dish, one that will keep its
shape during cooking, in
preference to a mealy variety,
which will break up easily
once cooked.

1 Place the garlic, ginger,
lemongrass, and coriander
seeds in a mortar and, using a pestle,
pound to a smooth paste.

2 Heat 2 tablespoons of the oil in a
skillet or preheated wok. Stir in
the garlic paste mixture and stir-fry for
30 seconds. Stir in the curry paste and
turmeric, then add the coconut milk
and bring to a boil.

3 Add the potatoes and stock.
Return to a boil, then reduce the
heat and let simmer, uncovered, for
10–12 minutes, or until the potatoes
are almost tender.

4 Stir in the spinach and let simmer
until the leaves are wilted.

5 Meanwhile, heat the remaining
oil in a separate skillet. Add the
onion and sauté until crisp and
golden brown.

6 Place the sautéed onions on top
of the curry just before serving.

187

vegetable biryani

serves four

1 large potato, cubed

3½ oz/100 g baby carrots

1¾ oz/50 g okra, thickly sliced

2 celery stalks, sliced

2¾ oz/75 g baby white
   mushrooms, halved

1 eggplant, halved and sliced

1¼ cups plain yogurt

1 tbsp grated fresh gingerroot

2 large onions, grated

4 garlic cloves, crushed

1 tsp ground turmeric

1 tbsp curry powder

2 tbsp butter

2 onions, sliced

generous 1 cup basmati rice

cilantro leaves, to garnish

1 Cook the potato cubes, carrots, and okra in a pan of lightly salted boiling water for 7–8 minutes. Drain well and place in a large bowl. Add the celery, mushrooms, and eggplant and mix together.

2 Mix the yogurt, ginger, grated onions, garlic, turmeric, and curry powder together in a separate bowl and spoon over the vegetables. Cover and let marinate in the refrigerator for at least 2 hours.

3 Preheat the oven to 375°F/190°C. Heat the butter in a skillet. Add the sliced onions and cook for 5–6 minutes, or until golden. Remove a few onions from the skillet and set aside for the garnish.

4 Add the marinated vegetables to the onions and cook for 10 minutes.

5 Cook the rice in a pan of boiling water for 7 minutes. Drain well and set on one side.

6 Place half the rice in an 8-cup ovenproof casserole. Spoon the vegetables on top and cover with the remaining rice. Cover and cook in the oven for 20–25 minutes, or until the rice is tender.

7 Spoon the biryani onto a warmed serving plate and garnish with the reserved onions and cilantro leaves, then serve at once.

spiced cashew curry

serves four

⅔ cup unsalted cashews

1 tsp coriander seeds

1 tsp cumin seeds

2 green cardamoms, crushed

1 tbsp corn oil

1 onion, thinly sliced

1 garlic clove, crushed

1 small fresh green chili, seeded
    and chopped

1 cinnamon stick

½ tsp ground turmeric

4 tbsp coconut cream

1¼ cups hot vegetable stock

3 kaffir lime leaves, finely shredded

boiled jasmine rice, to serve

COOK'S TIP

All spices give the best flavor
when freshly crushed, but if you
prefer, you can use ground spices
instead of crushing them yourself
in a mortar with a pestle.

1 Soak the cashews in cold water overnight. Drain thoroughly. Crush the coriander and cumin seeds and cardamoms with a pestle in a mortar.

2 Heat the oil in a skillet and stir-fry the onion and garlic for 2–3 minutes, or until softened but not browned. Add the chili, crushed spices, cinnamon stick, and turmeric and stir-fry for an additional minute.

3 Add the coconut cream and the hot stock to the skillet. Bring to a boil, then add the cashews and lime leaves.

4 Cover the skillet, reduce the heat, and let simmer for 20 minutes. Serve hot with jasmine rice.

coconut vegetable curry

serves four

1 large eggplant, cut into
  1-inch/2.5-cm cubes

salt and pepper

2 tbsp vegetable oil

2 garlic cloves, crushed

1 fresh green chili, seeded and
  finely chopped

1 tsp grated fresh gingerroot

1 onion, finely chopped

2 tsp garam masala

8 green cardamoms

1 tsp ground turmeric

1 tbsp tomato paste

3 cups vegetable stock

1 tbsp lemon juice

8 oz/225 g potatoes, diced

9 oz/250 g small cauliflower florets

8 oz/225 g okra

2 cups frozen peas

⅔ cup coconut milk

flaked coconut, to garnish

naan bread, to serve

1 Layer the eggplant in a bowl, sprinkling with salt as you go. Set aside for 30 minutes. Rinse well under cold running water. Drain and pat dry. Set aside.

2 Heat the oil in a large pan over medium heat and cook the garlic, chili, ginger, onion, and spices for 4–5 minutes.

3 Stir in the tomato paste, stock, lemon juice, potatoes, and cauliflower and mix well. Bring to a boil, then reduce the heat and let simmer, covered, for 15 minutes.

4 Stir in the eggplant, okra, peas, and coconut milk and season to taste with salt and pepper. Let simmer, uncovered, for 10 minutes, or until tender. Discard the cardamoms. Pile the curry onto a warmed serving plate, then garnish with flaked coconut and serve with naan bread.

mixed vegetable balti

serves four

scant 1 cup split yellow peas

3 tbsp vegetable oil

1 tsp onion seeds

2 onions, sliced

4 oz/115 g zucchini, sliced

4 oz/115 g potatoes, cut into

    ½-inch/1-cm cubes

4 oz/115 g carrots, sliced

1 small eggplant, sliced

8 oz/225 g tomatoes, chopped

1¼ cups water

3 garlic cloves, chopped

1 tsp ground cumin

1 tsp ground coriander

1 tsp salt

2 fresh green chilies, sliced

½ tsp garam masala

2 tbsp chopped cilantro

1 Put the split peas in a pan and cover with lightly salted water. Bring to a boil, then reduce the heat and let simmer for 30 minutes. Drain the peas and keep warm.

2 Heat the oil in a karahi or preheated wok, then add the onion seeds and sauté until they pop.

3 Add the onions and stir-fry over medium heat until golden brown.

4 Add the zucchini, potatoes, carrots, and eggplant to the pan. Stir-fry for 2 minutes.

5 Stir in the tomatoes, water, garlic, cumin, ground coriander, salt, chilies, garam masala, and the reserved split peas.

6 Bring to a boil, then reduce the heat and simmer for 15 minutes, or until all the vegetables are tender.

7 Stir the cilantro into the vegetables. Transfer to a warmed serving dish and serve at once.

mexican pickles

serves six

3 tbsp vegetable oil

1 onion, thinly sliced

5 garlic cloves, cut into slivers

3 carrots, thinly sliced

2 fresh green chilies, such as
  jalapeño or serrano, seeded and
  cut into strips

1 small cauliflower, broken
  into florets or cut into
  bite-size chunks

½ red bell pepper, seeded and diced
  or cut into strips

1 celery stalk, cut into
  bite-size pieces

½ tsp oregano leaves

1 bay leaf

¼ tsp ground cumin

5 tbsp cider vinegar

salt and pepper

1 Heat the oil in a heavy-bottom skillet and add the onion, garlic, carrots, chilies, cauliflower, bell pepper, and celery. Cook over low heat, stirring occasionally, for 3–4 minutes, or until just softened but not browned.

2 Add the oregano, bay leaf, cumin, and vinegar and season to taste with salt and pepper. Add just enough water to cover the vegetables. Cook for an additional 5–10 minutes, or just long enough for the vegetables to be tender but still firm to the bite.

3 Adjust the seasoning, adding more vinegar if needed. Set aside to cool and serve as a relish or with buttered tortillas Mexican-style. The Mexican pickles will keep for up to 2 weeks, if stored in a sealed container in the refrigerator.

COOK'S TIP
Wear rubber gloves when slicing and seeding fresh chilies, and do not touch your eyes during preparation.

spicy black-eye peas

serves four

2 cups black-eye peas, soaked
   overnight in cold water

1 tbsp vegetable oil

2 onions, chopped

1 tbsp honey

2 tbsp molasses

4 tbsp dark soy sauce

1 tsp dry mustard powder

4 tbsp tomato paste

2 cups vegetable stock

1 bay leaf

1 sprig each of fresh rosemary,
   thyme, and sage

1 small orange

pepper

1 tbsp cornstarch

2 red bell peppers, diced

2 tbsp chopped fresh parsley,
   to garnish

crusty bread, to serve

1 Preheat the oven to 300°F/150°C. Rinse the peas and place in a pan. Cover with water, then bring to a boil and boil rapidly for 10 minutes. Drain and place in an ovenproof casserole.

2 Meanwhile, heat the oil in a skillet and sauté the onions for 5 minutes. Stir in the honey, molasses, soy sauce, mustard, and tomato paste. Pour in the stock and bring to a boil, then pour over the peas.

3 Tie the bay leaf and herbs together with a clean piece of string and add to the casserole. Using a vegetable peeler, pare 3 pieces of orange rind and mix into the peas, along with plenty of pepper. Cover and bake in the oven for 1 hour.

4 Extract the juice from the orange and blend with the cornstarch to form a paste. Stir into the peas with the bell peppers. Cover and cook for an additional 1 hour, or until the sauce is rich and thick and the peas are tender. Discard the herbs and orange rind.

5 Garnish with chopped parsley and serve with crusty bread.

spanish tortilla

2 lb 4 oz/1 kg waxy potatoes,
    thinly sliced

4 tbsp vegetable oil

1 onion, sliced

2 garlic cloves, crushed

1 green bell pepper, diced

2 tomatoes, seeded and chopped

¼ cup canned corn kernels, drained

6 large eggs, beaten

2 tbsp chopped fresh parsley

salt and pepper

crisp salad, to serve

COOK'S TIP

Ensure that the handle of your skillet is heatproof before placing it under the broiler. Use an oven mitt when removing it because it will be very hot.

1 Parboil the potatoes in a pan of lightly salted boiling water for 5 minutes. Drain well.

2 Heat the oil in a large skillet, then add the potatoes and onion, and sauté over low heat, stirring constantly, for 5 minutes, or until the potatoes have browned.

3 Add the garlic, bell pepper, tomatoes, and corn, mixing well.

4 Pour in the eggs and add the parsley. Season to taste with salt and pepper. Cook for 10–12 minutes, or until the underside is cooked.

5 Preheat the broiler. Remove the skillet from the heat and continue to cook the tortilla under the hot broiler for 5–7 minutes, or until the tortilla is set and the top is golden brown.

6 Cut the tortilla into wedges or cubes, depending on your preference, and transfer to serving dishes. Serve hot, warm, or cold with a crisp salad.

winter vegetable cobbler

serves four

1 tbsp olive oil

1 garlic clove, crushed

8 small onions, halved

2 celery stalks, sliced

8 oz/225 g rutabaga, chopped

2 carrots, sliced

½ small cauliflower, broken
   into florets

8 oz/225 g mushrooms, sliced

14 oz/400 g canned
   chopped tomatoes

generous ¼ cup split red lentils,
   rinsed

2 tbsp cornstarch

3–4 tbsp water

1¼ cups vegetable stock

2 tsp Tabasco sauce

2 tsp chopped fresh oregano, plus
   extra sprigs to garnish

COBBLER TOPPING

1½ cups self-rising flour,
   plus extra for dusting

pinch of salt

4 tbsp butter

1 cup grated sharp Cheddar cheese

2 tsp chopped fresh oregano

1 egg, lightly beaten

⅔ cup milk

1 Preheat the oven to 350°F/
180°C. Heat the oil in a skillet
and cook the garlic and onions for
5 minutes. Add the celery, rutabaga,
carrots, and cauliflower and cook for
2–3 minutes. Add the mushrooms,
tomatoes, and lentils. Blend the
cornstarch with the water and stir into
the skillet with the stock, Tabasco
sauce, and oregano.

2 Transfer to an ovenproof dish,
then cover and bake in the oven
for 20 minutes.

3 To make the topping, sift the flour
with the salt into a bowl. Rub in
the butter, then stir in most of the
cheese and the oregano. Beat the egg
with the milk and add enough to the
dry ingredients to make a soft dough.
Knead, then roll out on a lightly floured
counter to ½ inch/1 cm thick and cut
into 2-inch/5-cm circles.

4 Remove the dish from the oven
and increase the temperature to
400°F/200°C. Arrange the biscuits
around the edge of the dish, brush
with the remaining egg and milk, and
sprinkle with the reserved cheese.
Bake for an additional 10–12 minutes.
Garnish with oregano and serve.

spicy potato & lemon casserole

serves four

generous ⅓ cup olive oil

2 red onions, cut into 8 wedges

3 garlic cloves, crushed

2 tsp ground cumin

2 tsp ground coriander

pinch of cayenne pepper

1 carrot, thickly sliced

2 small turnips, cut into fourths

1 zucchini, sliced

1 lb/450 g potatoes, thickly sliced

rind and juice of 2 large lemons

1¼ cups vegetable stock

salt and pepper

2 tbsp chopped cilantro

COOK'S TIP

A selection of spices and herbs is important for adding variety to your cooking—add to your range each time you try a new recipe.

Check the vegetables while cooking, because they may start to stick to the casserole. Add a little more boiling water or stock if necessary.

1 Heat the oil in an ovenproof casserole.

2 Add the onion wedges and sauté for 3 minutes, stirring.

3 Add the garlic and cook for 30 seconds. Mix in the spices and cook for 1 minute, stirring constantly.

4 Add the carrot, turnips, zucchini, and potatoes and stir to coat in the oil.

5 Add the lemon rind and juice, stock, and salt and pepper to taste, then cover and cook over medium heat for 20–30 minutes, stirring occasionally.

6 Remove the lid, then sprinkle in the cilantro and stir well. Serve at once.

pasta & bean casserole

1 Preheat the oven to 350°F/180°C.
Put the beans in a large pan, then
add water to cover and bring to a boil.
Boil rapidly for 20 minutes, then drain
and set aside.

2 Cook the pasta for 3 minutes only
in a large pan of lightly salted
boiling water, adding 1 tablespoon
of the oil. Drain in a strainer and
set aside.

3 Put the beans in a large,
ovenproof casserole, then pour in
the stock and stir in the remaining oil,
the onions, garlic, bay leaves, herbs,
wine, and tomato paste.

4 Bring to a boil, then cover the
casserole and cook in the oven
for 2 hours.

5 Remove the casserole from the
oven, then add the reserved
pasta, the celery, fennel, mushrooms,
and tomatoes and season to taste with
salt and pepper.

6 Stir in the sugar and sprinkle the
bread crumbs on top. Cover the
casserole again, then return to the
oven, and cook for an additional 1 hour.
Serve straight from the casserole with
salad greens and crusty bread.

lentil & rice casserole

serves four

1 cup split red lentils, rinsed

¼ cup long-grain rice

4 cups vegetable stock

⅔ cup dry white wine

1 leek, cut into chunks

3 garlic cloves, crushed

14 oz/400 g canned
    chopped tomatoes

1 tsp ground cumin

1 tsp chili powder

1 tsp garam masala

1 red bell pepper, seeded and sliced

3½ oz/100 g small broccoli florets

8 baby corn, halved lengthwise

⅓ cup halved green beans

1 tbsp shredded fresh basil, plus
    extra sprigs to garnish

salt and pepper

VARIATION

You can vary the rice in this
recipe—use brown or wild rice,
if you prefer.

1 Place the lentils, rice, stock, and
wine in an ovenproof casserole
over low heat and cook for
20 minutes, stirring occasionally.

2 Add the leek, garlic, tomatoes,
cumin, chili powder, garam
masala, pepper, broccoli, baby corn,
and beans.

3 Bring the mixture to a boil, then
reduce the heat and let simmer,
covered, for 10–15 minutes, or until
the vegetables are tender.

4 Add the shredded basil and
season to taste with salt
and pepper.

5 Garnish with basil sprigs and
serve at once.

chickpea & vegetable casserole

serves four

1 tbsp olive oil

1 red onion, halved and sliced

3 garlic cloves, crushed

5 cups fresh spinach leaves

1 fennel bulb, cut into eighths

1 red bell pepper, seeded and diced

1 tbsp all-purpose flour

2 cups vegetable stock

⅓ cup dry white wine

14 oz/400 g canned
    chickpeas, drained

1 bay leaf

1 tsp ground coriander

½ tsp paprika

salt and pepper

fennel fronds, to garnish

1 Heat the oil in a large, ovenproof casserole. Add the onion and garlic and sauté for 1 minute, stirring. Add the spinach and cook for 4 minutes, or until wilted.

2 Add the fennel and bell pepper and cook for 2 minutes, stirring.

3 Stir in the flour and cook for 1 minute.

4 Add the stock, wine, chickpeas, bay leaf, coriander, and paprika, then cover and cook for 30 minutes. Season to taste with salt and pepper, then garnish with fennel fronds and serve at once.

COOK'S TIP
Use other canned lentils or mixed beans instead of the chickpeas, if you prefer.

VARIATION
Replace the coriander with nutmeg, if you prefer, as it works particularly well with spinach.

vegetable hotchpotch

serves four

2 large potatoes, thinly sliced

2 tbsp vegetable oil

1 red onion, halved and sliced

1 leek, sliced

2 garlic cloves, crushed

1 carrot, cut into chunks

3½ oz/100 g broccoli florets

3½ oz/100 g cauliflower florets

2 small turnips, cut into fourths

1 tbsp all-purpose flour

3 cups vegetable stock

⅔ cup hard cider

1 eating apple, sliced

2 tbsp chopped fresh sage

pinch of cayenne pepper

salt and pepper

½ cup grated Cheddar cheese

1 Preheat the oven to 375°F/ 190°C. Cook the potato slices in a pan of boiling water for 10 minutes. Drain thoroughly and set aside until required.

2 Heat the oil in an ovenproof casserole. Add the onion, leek, and garlic and sauté for 2–3 minutes. Add the remaining vegetables and cook for 3–4 minutes, stirring.

3 Stir in the flour and cook for 1 minute. Gradually add the stock and cider and bring the mixture to a boil. Add the apple, sage, and cayenne pepper and season well with salt and pepper. Remove the casserole from the heat. Transfer the vegetables to an ovenproof dish.

COOK'S TIP

If the potato starts to brown too quickly, cover with foil for the last 10 minutes of the cooking time to prevent the top burning.

4 Arrange the potato slices on top of the vegetable mixture to cover.

5 Sprinkle the cheese on top of the potato slices and cook in the oven for 30–35 minutes, or until the potato is golden brown and starting to crisp slightly around the edges. Serve at once.

sweet & sour eggplants

serves four

2 large eggplants

salt and pepper

6 tbsp olive oil

4 garlic cloves, crushed

1 onion, cut into 8 wedges

4 large tomatoes, seeded
and chopped

3 tbsp chopped fresh mint

⅔ cup vegetable stock

4 tsp brown sugar

2 tbsp red wine vinegar

1 tsp dried red pepper flakes

fresh mint sprigs, to garnish

1 Using a sharp knife, cut the eggplants into cubes. Place them in a strainer, then sprinkle with salt and let stand for 30 minutes. Rinse thoroughly under cold running water and drain well. This process removes all the bitter juices from the eggplants. Pat dry with paper towels.

2 Heat the oil in a large skillet. Add the eggplant and sauté, stirring constantly, for 1–2 minutes.

3 Stir in the garlic and onion and cook for 2–3 minutes.

4 Stir in the tomatoes, mint, and stock, then cover and cook for 15–20 minutes, or until the vegetables are tender.

5 Stir in the sugar, vinegar, and red pepper flakes, then season to taste with salt and pepper and cook for 2–3 minutes. Transfer the eggplants to warmed serving plates and garnish with mint sprigs, then serve.

COOK'S TIP

Mint is a popular herb in Middle Eastern cooking. It is a useful herb to grow yourself, as it can be added to a variety of dishes, particularly salads and vegetable dishes. It can be grown easily in a garden or window box.

cauliflower bake

serves four

1 lb/450 g cauliflower, broken
    into florets

2 large potatoes, cubed

3½ oz/100 g cherry tomatoes

SAUCE

2 tbsp butter or margarine

1 leek, sliced

1 garlic clove, crushed

2 tbsp all-purpose flour

1¼ cups milk

scant ¾ cup mixed grated cheese,
    such as Cheddar, Parmesan,
    and Gruyère cheese

½ tsp paprika

2 tbsp chopped fresh flatleaf
    parsley, plus extra to garnish

salt and pepper

1 Preheat the oven to 350°F/
180°C. Cook the cauliflower in
a pan of boiling water for 10 minutes.
Drain well and set aside. Meanwhile,
cook the potatoes in a separate pan
of boiling water for 10 minutes, drain,
and set aside.

2 To make the sauce, melt the
butter or margarine in a pan.
Add the leek and garlic and sauté for
1 minute. Add the flour and cook
for 1 minute. Remove the pan from
the heat and gradually stir in the milk,
scant ½ cup of the cheese, the paprika,
and parsley. Return the pan to the
heat. Bring to a boil, stirring. Season
to taste with salt and pepper.

3 Spoon the cauliflower into a
deep, ovenproof dish. Add the
tomatoes and top with the potatoes.
Pour the sauce over the potatoes and
sprinkle over the remaining cheese.

4 Cook in the oven for 20 minutes,
or until the vegetables are cooked
through and the cheese is golden
brown and bubbling. Garnish with
parsley and serve at once.

VARIATION

This dish could be made with
broccoli instead of the
cauliflower as an alternative.

cheese & potato layer bake

serves four

1 lb/450 g potatoes

salt and pepper

1 leek, sliced

3 garlic cloves, crushed

scant ½ cup grated Cheddar cheese

1¾ oz/50 g mozzarella
   cheese, grated

¼ cup freshly grated
   Parmesan cheese

2 tbsp chopped fresh flatleaf
   parsley, plus extra to garnish

⅔ cup light cream

⅔ cup milk

1 Preheat the oven to 325°F/160°C. Cook the potatoes in a pan of lightly salted boiling water for 10 minutes. Drain well.

2 Cut the potatoes into thin slices. Arrange a layer of potatoes in the bottom of an ovenproof dish. Layer with a little of the leek, garlic, cheeses, and chopped parsley and season well with salt and pepper.

3 Repeat the layers until all of the ingredients have been used, finishing with a layer of cheese on top.

4 Mix the cream and milk together and season to taste with salt and pepper, then pour the mixture over the potato layers.

5 Cook in the oven for 1–1¼ hours, or until the cheese is golden brown and bubbling and the potatoes are cooked through.

6 Garnish with chopped parsley and serve at once.

COOK'S TIP

This tasty bake is perfect for serving as an accompaniment to a whole range of main dishes featured in the book, which can be cooked in the oven at the same time, such as a meat or poultry casserole or a gently baked fish dish.

vegetable toad-in-the-hole

serves four

BATTER

scant ¾ cup all-purpose flour

pinch of salt

2 eggs, beaten

scant 1 cup milk

2 tbsp whole-grain mustard

2 tbsp vegetable oil

FILLING

2¾ oz/75 g baby carrots,
  halved lengthwise

1¾ oz/50 g green beans

2 tbsp butter

2 garlic cloves, crushed

1 onion, cut into 8 wedges

scant ½ cup canned corn
  kernels, drained

2 tomatoes, seeded and cut
  into chunks

1 tsp whole-grain mustard

1 tbsp chopped fresh mixed herbs

salt and pepper

COOK'S TIP

It is important that the oil is hot
before adding the batter so that
the batter starts to cook and
rise immediately.

1 Preheat the oven to
400°F/200°C. To make the
batter, sift the flour and the salt
into a large bowl. Make a well in
the center and beat in the eggs
and milk to form a batter. Stir in
the mustard and let the batter stand
until required.

2 Pour the oil into a shallow
ovenproof dish and heat in the
oven for 10 minutes.

3 To make the filling, cook the
carrots and beans in a pan of
boiling water for 7 minutes, or until
tender. Drain well. Melt the butter in
a skillet. Add the garlic and onion and
sauté for 2 minutes, stirring.

4 Add the corn, tomatoes, mustard,
and herbs. Season well with
salt and pepper and add the carrots
and beans.

5 Remove the dish from the oven
and pour in the batter. Spoon
the vegetables into the center, then
return to the oven and cook for
30–35 minutes, or until the batter
has risen and set. Serve at once.

cauliflower & broccoli with herb sauce

serves four

2 baby cauliflowers

8 oz/225 g broccoli

salt and pepper

SAUCE

8 tbsp olive oil

4 tbsp butter

2 tsp grated fresh gingerroot

rind and juice of 2 lemons

5 tbsp chopped cilantro

5 tbsp grated Cheddar cheese

1 Preheat the broiler to medium. Using a sharp knife, cut the cauliflowers in half and the broccoli into very large florets.

2 Cook the cauliflower and broccoli in a pan of lightly salted boiling water for 10 minutes. Drain well, then transfer to a shallow ovenproof dish and keep warm until required.

3 To make the sauce, place the oil and butter in a skillet and heat gently until the butter melts. Add the ginger, lemon rind and juice, and cilantro and let simmer for 2–3 minutes, stirring occasionally.

4 Season the sauce with salt and pepper to taste, then pour over the vegetables in the dish and sprinkle the cheese on top.

5 Cook under the hot broiler for 2–3 minutes, or until the cheese is bubbling and golden. Let cool for 1–2 minutes, then serve.

VARIATION

Lime or orange could be used instead of the lemon for a fruity and refreshing sauce.

green tagliatelle with garlic

serves four

2 tbsp walnut oil

1 bunch scallions, sliced

2 garlic cloves, thinly sliced

8 oz/225 g sliced mushrooms

salt and pepper

1 lb/450 g fresh green and
white tagliatelle

generous 1 cup frozen spinach,
thawed and drained

½ cup full-fat soft cheese with garlic
and herbs

4 tbsp light cream

scant ½ cup unsalted pistachios,
chopped

2 tbsp shredded fresh basil

fresh basil sprigs, to garnish

Italian bread, to serve

1 Heat the oil in a large skillet. Add the scallions and garlic and cook for 1 minute, or until just softened.

2 Add the mushrooms to the skillet and stir well. Cover and cook over low heat for about 5 minutes, or until just softened but not browned.

3 Meanwhile, bring a large pan of lightly salted water to a boil. Add the tagliatelle, then return to a boil and cook for 3–5 minutes, or until tender but still firm to the bite. Drain the tagliatelle thoroughly and return to the pan.

4 Add the spinach to the skillet and heat through for 1–2 minutes. Add the cheese to the skillet and heat until slightly melted. Stir in the cream and cook, without letting the mixture come to a boil, until warmed through.

5 Pour the sauce over the pasta, season to taste with salt and pepper, and mix well. Heat through gently, stirring constantly, for 2–3 minutes.

6 Transfer the pasta to a warmed serving dish and sprinkle with the pistachios and shredded basil. Garnish with basil sprigs and serve at once with focaccia, ciabatta, or other Italian bread of your choice.

baked cheese & tomato macaroni

serves four

2 cups dried elbow macaroni

salt and pepper

1½ cups grated Cheddar cheese

scant 1 cup freshly grated
   Parmesan cheese

1 tbsp butter or margarine, plus
   extra for greasing

4 tbsp fresh white bread crumbs

1 tbsp chopped fresh basil

TOMATO SAUCE

1 tbsp olive oil

1 shallot, finely chopped

2 garlic cloves, crushed

1 lb/450 g canned
   chopped tomatoes

1 tbsp chopped fresh basil

salt and pepper

COOK'S TIP

Use other dried pasta shapes,
such as penne, if you have them
to hand, instead of the macaroni.

1 Preheat the oven to 375°F/
190°C. To make the tomato
sauce, heat the oil in a pan. Add
the shallot and garlic and sauté for
1 minute. Add the tomatoes, basil, and
salt and pepper to taste and cook over
medium heat, stirring, for 10 minutes.

2 Meanwhile, cook the macaroni
in a large pan of lightly salted
boiling water for 8 minutes, or until
just undercooked. Drain.

3 Mix both of the cheeses together
in a bowl.

4 Grease a deep, ovenproof dish.
Spoon a third of the tomato sauce
into the bottom of the dish and top
with a third of the macaroni, and then
a third of the cheeses. Season to taste
with salt and pepper. Repeat the layers
twice more.

5 Mix the bread crumbs and basil
together and sprinkle over the
top. Dot with the butter or margarine
and cook in the oven for 25 minutes,
or until golden brown and bubbling.
Serve at once.

vegetable lasagna

serves four

1 eggplant, sliced

salt and pepper

3 tbsp olive oil

2 garlic cloves, crushed

1 red onion, halved and sliced

1 green bell pepper, seeded
    and diced

1 red bell pepper, seeded and diced

1 yellow bell pepper, seeded
    and diced

8 oz/225 g mushrooms, sliced

2 celery stalks, sliced

1 zucchini, diced

½ tsp chili powder

½ tsp ground cumin

2 tomatoes, chopped

1¼ cups strained tomatoes

2 tbsp chopped fresh basil

8 no-precook lasagna verde sheets

CHEESE SAUCE

2 tbsp butter or margarine

1 tbsp all-purpose flour

⅔ cup vegetable stock

1¼ cups milk

scant ¾ cup grated Cheddar cheese

1 tsp Dijon mustard

1 tbsp chopped fresh basil

1 egg, beaten

1 Preheat the oven to 350°F/
180°C. Place the eggplant
slices in a strainer, then sprinkle with
salt, and let stand for 20 minutes.
Rinse under cold running water, then
drain and set aside.

2 Heat the oil in a large skillet.
Add the garlic and onion and
sauté for 1–2 minutes. Add the bell
peppers, mushrooms, celery, and
zucchini and cook for 3–4 minutes,
stirring. Stir in the spices and cook for
1 minute.

3 Mix the tomatoes, strained
tomatoes, and basil together,
then season well with salt and pepper.

4 To make the sauce, melt the
butter or margarine in a pan.
Add the flour and cook for 1 minute.
Remove the pan from the heat and
stir in the stock and milk. Return to
the heat and add half the cheese
and mustard. Boil, stirring, until
thickened. Stir in the basil and season
to taste with salt and pepper. Remove
the pan from the heat and stir in the
egg. Place half the lasagna sheets in
an ovenproof dish. Top with half the
vegetables, then half the tomato
sauce. Cover with half the eggplants.
Repeat and spoon the cheese sauce
on top. Sprinkle with the remaining
cheese and cook in the oven for
40 minutes. Serve at once.

Fish

The range of seafood available these days is immense, but sometimes it is difficult to know how to cook unfamiliar fish. The answer might be to put it in a pot and make a fabulous stew. Creole Jambalaya (see page 232), Spanish Fish Stew (see page 250), or Bouillabaisse (see page 236) are as different as their countries of origin, equally delicious, and incredibly easy to make. Another answer might be to stir it with rice to make an elegant Shrimp and Asparagus Risotto (see page 231) or to combine it with chili and other spices in a one-pot Goan Fish Curry (see page 234). Then, again, there are soups and chowders, bakes, and pasta dishes—and no unhealthy french fries in sight. There are recipes for inexpensive family meals and dishes for sophisticated entertaining featuring seafood of all kinds, from cod to crab and from sardines to squid—even a lobster one-pot.

cullen skink

serves four

8 oz/225 g undyed smoked
    haddock fillet

2 tbsp butter

1 onion, finely chopped

2½ cups milk

12 oz/350 g potatoes, diced

12 oz/350 g cod, boned, skinned,
    and cubed

⅔ cup heavy cream

2 tbsp chopped fresh parsley

salt and pepper

lemon juice, to taste

TO GARNISH

lemon slices

parsley sprigs

1 Put the haddock fillet in a large skillet and cover with boiling water. Let stand for 10 minutes. Drain, reserving 1¼ cups of the soaking water. Flake the fish, taking care to remove all the bones.

2 Heat the butter in a large pan over low heat. Add the onion and cook for 10 minutes, or until softened. Add the milk and bring to a gentle simmer before adding the potatoes. Cook for 10 minutes.

3 Add the reserved haddock and cod. Let simmer for an additional 10 minutes, or until the cod is tender.

COOK'S TIP

Look for Finnan haddock, if you can find it. Do not use yellow-dyed haddock fillet, which is often actually whiting and not haddock at all.

4 Remove one-third of the fish and potatoes, then transfer to a food processor and blend until smooth. Alternatively, push through a strainer into a bowl. Return to the pan with the cream, parsley, and salt and pepper to taste. Taste and add lemon juice, if wished. Add a little of the reserved soaking water if the soup seems too thick. Reheat and serve, garnished with lemon slices and parsley sprigs.

mediterranean fish soup

serves four

1 tbsp olive oil

1 large onion, chopped

2 garlic cloves, finely chopped

2 cups fish stock

⅔ cup dry white wine

1 bay leaf

1 sprig each of fresh thyme, rosemary, and oregano

1 lb/450 g firm white fish fillets, such as cod, angler fish, or halibut, skinned and cut into 1-inch/2.5-cm cubes

1 lb/450 g live mussels, scrubbed and debearded

14 oz/400 g canned chopped tomatoes

8 oz/225 g cooked shelled shrimp, thawed if frozen

salt and pepper

fresh thyme sprigs, to garnish

TO SERVE

lemon wedges

4 slices toasted French bread, rubbed with a cut garlic clove

1 Heat the oil in a large, heavy-bottom pan over medium heat and sauté the onion and garlic for 2–3 minutes, or until just softened.

2 Pour in the stock and wine and bring to a boil.

3 Tie the bay leaf and herbs together with a clean piece of string and add to the pan with the fish and mussels. Stir, then cover and let simmer for 5 minutes.

4 Stir in the tomatoes and shrimp and cook for an additional 3–4 minutes, or until piping hot and the fish is cooked through.

5 Discard the herbs and any mussels that have not opened. Season to taste with salt and pepper, then ladle into warmed soup bowls.

6 Garnish with thyme sprigs and serve with lemon wedges and toasted bread rubbed with garlic.

mexican fish & roasted tomato soup

serves four

5 ripe tomatoes

5 garlic cloves, unpeeled

1 lb 2 oz/500 g red snapper, cut
    into chunks

4 cups fish stock or water mixed
    with 1–2 fish bouillon cubes

2–3 tbsp olive oil

1 onion, chopped

2 fresh green chilies, such as
    serrano, seeded and
    thinly sliced

lime wedges, to serve

1 Heat a dry, heavy-bottom skillet over high heat. Add the tomatoes and garlic and cook until the skins are blackened and the flesh is tender. Alternatively, cook under a preheated hot broiler, or place the tomatoes and garlic in a roasting pan and bake in a preheated oven at 375°F/190°C for 40 minutes.

2 Let the tomatoes and garlic cool, then remove the skins and coarsely chop, combining them with any juices from the skillet or broiler pan or roasting pan. Set aside.

3 Poach the fish in the stock in a deep skillet or pan over medium heat until it is just opaque and slightly firm. Remove from the heat and set aside.

4 Heat the oil in a separate deep skillet or pan. Add the onion and cook for 5 minutes, or until softened. Strain in the cooking liquid from the fish, then stir in the tomatoes and garlic.

5 Bring to a boil, then reduce the heat and let simmer for 5 minutes to combine the flavors. Add the chilies.

6 Divide chunks of the poached fish between soup bowls and ladle over the hot soup. Serve with lime wedges for squeezing over the top.

thai fish soup

serves four

2 cups light chicken stock

2 kaffir lime leaves, chopped

2-inch/5-cm piece fresh lemongrass, chopped

3 tbsp lemon juice

3 tbsp Thai fish sauce

2 small hot fresh green chilies, seeded and finely chopped

½ tsp sugar

8 small shiitake mushrooms, halved

1 lb/450 g raw shrimp, shelled if necessary and deveined

scallions, to garnish

TOM YAM SAUCE

4 tbsp vegetable oil

5 garlic cloves, finely chopped

1 large shallot, finely chopped

2 large hot dried red chilies, chopped

1 tbsp dried shrimp (optional)

1 tbsp Thai fish sauce

2 tsp sugar

1 First make the tom yam sauce. Heat the oil in a small pan. Cook the garlic briefly until just brown, then remove with a slotted spoon and set aside. Cook the shallot in the oil until brown and crisp and remove with a slotted spoon. Add the dried chilies and sauté until they darken. Remove and drain on paper towels, reserving the oil for later use.

2 In a small food processor or spice grinder, grind the dried shrimp, if using, then add the reserved chilies, garlic, and shallot. Grind to a smooth paste. Return the paste to the original pan over low heat. Mix in the fish sauce and sugar, then remove from the heat.

COOK'S TIP

Ready-made tom yam sauce in jars can be bought from some Asian supermarkets.

3 Heat the stock and 2 tablespoons of the sauce in a large pan. Add the lime leaves, lemongrass, lemon juice, fish sauce, fresh chilies, and sugar. Let simmer for 2 minutes.

4 Add the mushrooms and shrimp and cook for an additional 2–3 minutes, or until the shrimp are cooked. Ladle the soup into warmed bowls and serve at once, garnished with scallions.

chinese crab & corn soup

serves four

1 tbsp vegetable oil

1 small onion, finely chopped

1 garlic clove, finely chopped

1 tsp grated fresh gingerroot

1 small fresh red chili, seeded and
  finely chopped

2 tbsp dry sherry or Chinese
  rice wine

8 oz/225 g fresh white crabmeat

11½ oz/325 g canned corn
  kernels, drained

2½ cups light chicken stock

1 tbsp light soy sauce

2 tbsp chopped cilantro

salt and pepper

2 eggs, beaten

chili "flowers," to garnish

2 Heat the oil in a large pan and
add the onion. Cook gently for
5 minutes, or until softened. Add the
garlic, ginger, and chili and cook gently
for an additional minute.

3 Add the sherry and bubble
until reduced by half. Add the
crabmeat, corn, stock, and soy sauce.
Bring to a boil, then let simmer for
5 minutes. Stir in the cilantro and salt
and pepper to taste.

4 Remove from the heat and
pour in the eggs. Wait for a
few seconds, then stir well to break
the eggs into ribbons. Serve the
soup at once, garnished with the
chili "flowers."

1 To make chili "flowers", hold the
stem of each chili with your
fingertips and use a small sharp,
pointed knife to cut a slit from down
the length from near the stem end to
the tip. Turn about a quarter turn and
make another cut. Repeat to make a
total of 4 cuts, then scrape out the
seeds. Cut each "petal" again, in half
or into quarters, to make 8–16 petals.
Place in ice water.

seafood stew

serves four–six

8 oz/225 g live clams

1 lb 9 oz/700 g mixed fish, such as
    sea bass, skate, red snapper,
    and rockfish

12–18 raw jumbo shrimp

about 3 tbsp olive oil

1 large onion, finely chopped

2 garlic cloves, very finely chopped

2 tomatoes, halved, seeded,
    and chopped

3 cups good quality, ready-made
    chilled fish stock

1 tbsp tomato paste

1 tsp fresh thyme leaves

pinch of saffron threads

pinch of sugar

salt and pepper

finely chopped fresh parsley,
    to garnish

1 Soak the clams in a bowl of lightly salted cold water for 30 minutes. Rinse them under cold running water and lightly scrub to remove any sand from the shells. Discard any broken clams or open clams that do not shut when firmly tapped with the back of a knife, because these will be unsafe to eat.

2 Prepare the fish as necessary, removing any skin and bones, then cut into bite-size chunks.

3 To prepare the shrimp, break off the heads. Peel off the shells, leaving the tails intact, if wished. Using a small knife, make a slit along the back of each and remove the thin black vein. Set all the seafood aside.

4 Heat the oil in a large pan. Add the onion and cook for 5 minutes, stirring. Add the garlic and cook for an additional 2 minutes, or until the onion is softened but not brown.

5 Add the tomatoes, stock, tomato paste, thyme, saffron, and sugar, then bring to a boil, stirring to dissolve the tomato paste. Reduce the heat, then cover and let simmer for 15 minutes. Season to taste with salt and pepper.

6 Add the seafood and let simmer until the clams open and the fish flakes easily. Discard any clams that do not open. Garnish with parsley and serve at once.

shrimp in green bean sauce

serves four

2 tbsp vegetable oil

3 onions, chopped

5 garlic cloves, chopped

5–7 ripe tomatoes, diced

6–8 oz/175–225 g green beans,
    cut into 2-inch/5-cm pieces and
    blanched for 1 minute

¼ tsp ground cumin

pinch of ground allspice

pinch of ground cinnamon

½–1 canned chipotle chili in
    adobo marinade, with some of
    the marinade

2 cups fish stock or water mixed
    with 1 fish bouillon cube

1 lb/450 g raw shrimp, shelled
    and deveined

cilantro sprigs, to garnish

1 lime, cut into wedges,
    to serve (optional)

VARIATION

If you can find them, use bottled
nopales (edible cactus), cut into
strips, to add an exotic touch
to the dish.

1 Heat the oil in a large, deep skillet. Add the onions and garlic and cook over low heat for 5–10 minutes, or until softened. Add the tomatoes and cook for an additional 2 minutes.

2 Add the beans, cumin, allspice, cinnamon, chili and marinade, and stock. Bring to a boil, then reduce the heat and let simmer for a few minutes to combine the flavors.

3 Add the shrimp and cook for 1–2 minutes only, then remove the skillet from the heat and let the shrimp steep in the hot liquid to finish cooking. They are cooked when they have turned a bright pink color.

4 Serve the shrimp at once, garnished with the cilantro sprigs and accompanied by the lime wedges, if wished.

squid simmered with tomatoes & olives

serves four

3 tbsp virgin olive oil

2 lb/900 g cleaned squid, cut into
   rings and tentacles

salt and pepper

1 onion, chopped

3 garlic cloves, chopped

14 oz/400 g canned chopped
   tomatoes

½–1 fresh mild–medium green chili,
   seeded and chopped

1 tbsp finely chopped fresh parsley

¼ tsp chopped fresh thyme

¼ tsp chopped fresh oregano

¼ tsp chopped fresh marjoram

large pinch of ground cinnamon

large pinch of ground allspice

large pinch of sugar

15–20 pimiento-stuffed green
   olives, sliced

1 tbsp capers

1 tbsp chopped cilantro, to garnish

1 Heat the oil in a deep, heavy-bottom skillet. Add the squid and lightly cook until it turns opaque. Season to taste with salt and pepper and remove from the skillet with a slotted spoon. Set aside in a bowl.

2 Add the onion and garlic to the remaining oil in the skillet and cook for 5 minutes, or until softened. Stir in the tomatoes, chili, herbs, cinnamon, allspice, sugar, and olives. Cover and cook over medium–low heat for 5–10 minutes, or until the mixture thickens slightly. Uncover the skillet and cook for an additional 5 minutes to concentrate the flavors.

3 Stir in the reserved squid and any of the juices that have gathered in the bowl. Add the capers to the mixture and heat through.

4 Taste and adjust the seasoning, then serve at once, garnished with cilantro.

mussels marinara

serves four

4 lb 8 oz/2 kg live mussels

4 tbsp olive oil

4–6 large garlic cloves, halved

1 lb 12 oz/800 g canned
   chopped tomatoes

1¼ cups dry white wine

2 tbsp finely chopped fresh
   flatleaf parsley, plus extra
   to garnish

1 tbsp finely chopped fresh oregano

salt and pepper

French bread, to serve

1 Soak the mussels in a bowl of lightly salted cold water for 30 minutes. Rinse them under cold running water and lightly scrub to remove any sand from the shells. Using a small, sharp knife, remove the "beards" from the shells.

2 Discard any broken mussels or open mussels that do not shut when firmly tapped with the back of a knife. This indicates they are dead and could cause food poisoning if eaten. Rinse the mussels again, then set aside in a strainer.

3 Heat the oil in a large pan or pot over medium–high heat. Add the garlic and cook, stirring, for 3 minutes. Using a slotted spoon, remove the garlic from the pan.

4 Add the tomatoes and their juice, the wine, parsley, and oregano and bring to a boil, stirring. Reduce the heat, then cover and let simmer for 5 minutes so that the flavors blend.

5 Add the mussels, cover the pan, and let simmer for 5–8 minutes, shaking the pan regularly, until the mussels open. Using a slotted spoon, transfer the mussels to serving bowls, discarding any that remain closed.

6 Season the sauce to taste with salt and pepper. Ladle the sauce over the mussels and sprinkle with extra chopped parsley, then serve at once with plenty of fresh French bread to mop up the delicious juices.

seafood rice

serves four–six

4 tbsp olive oil

16 large raw shrimp, shelled

8 oz/225 g cleaned squid, sliced

2 green bell peppers, seeded and
cut into strips

1 large onion, finely chopped

4 garlic cloves, finely chopped

2 bay leaves

1 tsp saffron threads

½ tsp crushed dried chilies

scant 2 cups risotto rice

1 cup dry white wine

3½ cups fish or chicken stock

salt and pepper

12–16 live clams, scrubbed

12–16 large live mussels, scrubbed
and debearded

2 tbsp chopped fresh
flatleaf parsley

RED BELL PEPPER SAUCE

2–3 tbsp olive oil

2 onions, finely chopped

4–6 garlic cloves, finely chopped

4–6 Italian roasted red bell peppers
in olive oil

14 oz/400 g canned
chopped tomatoes

1–1½ tsp hot paprika

1 To make the sauce, heat the oil in a skillet over medium heat. Add the onions and cook for 6–8 minutes, or until golden. Add the garlic and cook for 1 minute. Add the remaining ingredients and let simmer, stirring occasionally, for 10 minutes. Process in a food processor until smooth. Set aside and keep warm.

2 Heat half the oil in a wide skillet over high heat. Add the shrimp and stir-fry for 2 minutes, or until pink. Transfer to a plate. Add the squid and stir-fry for 2 minutes, or until just firm. Set aside with the shrimp.

3 Heat the remaining oil in the skillet. Add the bell peppers and onion, and stir-fry for 6 minutes, or until just tender. Stir in the garlic, bay leaves, saffron, and chilies and cook for 30 seconds. Add the rice and cook, stirring, until thoroughly coated.

4 Add the wine and stir until absorbed. Add the stock and salt and pepper to taste. Bring to a boil. Reduce the heat, cover, and let simmer for 20 minutes, or until the rice is just tender and the liquid almost absorbed.

5 Add the clams and mussels, then cover and cook for 10 minutes, or until the shells open. Discard any that remain closed. Stir in the shrimp and squid. Cover and heat through gently. Sprinkle with the chopped parsley and serve at once with the red bell pepper sauce.

shrimp & asparagus risotto

serves four

5 cups vegetable stock

12 oz/350 g asparagus, cut
  into 2-inch/5-cm lengths

2 tbsp olive oil

1 onion, finely chopped

1 garlic clove, finely chopped

generous 1½ cups risotto rice

1 lb/450 g raw jumbo shrimp,
  shelled and deveined

2 tbsp olive paste or tapenade

2 tbsp chopped fresh basil

salt and pepper

Parmesan cheese shavings,
  to garnish

1 Bring the stock to a boil in
  a large pan. Add the asparagus
and cook for 3 minutes, or until just
tender. Strain, reserving the stock, and
refresh under cold running water. Drain
and set aside.

COOK'S TIP

Use a vegetable peeler to make
shavings quickly and easily from
a piece of Parmesan cheese
for the garnish.

2 Heat the oil in a large, heavy-
  bottom skillet. Add the onion
and cook over low heat, stirring
occasionally, for 5 minutes, or until
softened. Add the garlic and cook
for an additional 30 seconds. Add the
rice and cook, stirring constantly, for
1–2 minutes, or until coated with the
oil and slightly translucent.

3 Keep the stock on low heat.
  Increase the heat under the
skillet to medium and start adding
the stock, a ladleful at a time, stirring
well between additions. Continue
until almost all the stock has been
absorbed. This should take
20–25 minutes.

4 Add the shrimp and asparagus
  with the last ladleful of stock and
cook for an additional 5 minutes, or
until the shrimp and rice are tender
and the stock has been absorbed.
Remove from the heat.

5 Stir in the olive paste, basil, and
  salt and pepper to taste. Set aside
for 1 minute. Garnish with Parmesan
and serve.

creole jambalaya

serves six–eight

2 tbsp vegetable oil

3 oz/85 g smoked ham, cut into
bite-size pieces

3 oz/85 g andouille or other smoked
pork sausage, cut into chunks

2 large onions, finely chopped

3–4 celery stalks, finely chopped

2 green bell peppers, seeded
and diced

2 garlic cloves, finely chopped

8 oz/225 g skinless, boneless
chicken breasts or thighs, cut
into pieces

4 tomatoes, peeled and chopped

¾ cup strained tomatoes

2 cups fish stock

2 cups long-grain rice

4 scallions, thickly sliced

9 oz/250 g raw shrimp, shelled

9 oz/250 g cooked white crabmeat

12 oysters, shelled, with their liquor

SEASONING MIX

2 dried bay leaves

1 tsp salt

1½–2 tsp cayenne pepper

1½ tsp dried oregano

1 tsp ground white pepper

1 tsp black pepper

1 To make the seasoning mix, combine all the ingredients in a bowl until well mixed.

2 Heat the oil in an ovenproof casserole over medium heat. Add the ham and sausage and cook for 8 minutes, stirring frequently, until golden. Using a slotted spoon, transfer to a large plate.

3 Add the onions, celery, and bell peppers to the casserole and cook for 4 minutes, or until just softened. Stir in the chopped garlic, then remove and set aside.

4 Add the chicken to the casserole and cook for 3–4 minutes, or until starting to color. Stir in the seasoning mix to coat. Return the ham, sausage, and vegetables to the casserole and stir to combine. Add the tomatoes and strained tomatoes, then pour in the stock. Bring to a boil.

5 Stir in the rice, then reduce the heat and let simmer, covered, for 12 minutes. Stir in the scallions and shrimp, cover, and cook for 4 minutes.

6 Gently stir in the crabmeat and oysters with their liquor. Cook until the rice is just tender. Remove from the heat and let stand, covered, for about 3 minutes before serving.

goan fish curry

serves four

1 lb 10 oz/750 g angler fish fillet,
cut into chunks

1 tbsp cider vinegar

1 tsp salt

1 tsp ground turmeric

3 tbsp vegetable oil

2 garlic cloves, crushed

1 small onion, finely chopped

2 tsp ground coriander

1 tsp cayenne pepper

2 tsp paprika

2 tbsp tamarind pulp plus 2 tbsp
boiling water (see Step 4)

3 oz/85 g creamed coconut,
cut into pieces

1¼ cups warm water

plain boiled rice, to serve

1 Put the fish on a plate and drizzle the vinegar over it. Combine half the salt and half the turmeric and sprinkle evenly over the fish. Cover and set aside for 20 minutes.

2 Heat the oil in a heavy-bottom skillet and add the garlic. Brown slightly, then add the onion and cook, stirring occasionally, for 3–4 minutes, or until softened but not browned. Add the ground coriander and stir-fry for 1 minute.

3 Mix the remaining turmeric, cayenne pepper, and paprika with about 2 tablespoons of water to make a paste. Add to the skillet and cook over low heat for 1–2 minutes.

COOK'S TIP

Tamarind, usually sold in blocks of dried pulp, imparts a sour yet slightly sweet flavor to curries.

4 In a heatproof bowl, stir the tamarind and boiling water together. When thickened and the pulp has separated from the seeds, rub through a strainer. Discard the seeds.

5 Add the coconut cream, warm water, and tamarind paste to the skillet and stir until the coconut has dissolved. Add the fish and any juices on the plate and let simmer gently for 4–5 minutes, or until the sauce has thickened and the fish is just tender. Serve on a bed of plain boiled rice.

thai green fish curry

serves four

2 tbsp vegetable oil

1 garlic clove, chopped

1 small eggplant, diced

½ cup coconut cream

2 tbsp Thai fish sauce

1 tsp sugar

8 oz/225 g firm white fish, cut into
   pieces, such as cod, haddock,
   or halibut

½ cup fish stock

2 kaffir lime leaves, finely shredded

about 15 leaves fresh Thai basil or
   ordinary basil

plain boiled rice or noodles, to serve

GREEN CURRY PASTE

5 fresh green chilies, seeded
   and chopped

2 tsp chopped lemongrass stems

1 large shallot, chopped

2 garlic cloves, chopped

1 tsp grated fresh gingerroot
   or galangal

2 cilantro sprigs, chopped

½ tsp ground coriander

¼ tsp ground cumin

1 kaffir lime leaf, finely chopped

½ tsp salt

1 To make the curry paste, put all the ingredients into a food processor or spice grinder and blend to a smooth paste, adding a little water if necessary. Alternatively, pound together all the ingredients, using a mortar and pestle, until smooth. Set the curry paste aside.

2 Heat the oil in a skillet or wok until almost smoking. Add the garlic and sauté until golden. Add the curry paste and stir-fry for a few seconds. Add the eggplant and stir-fry for 4–5 minutes, or until softened.

3 Add the coconut cream. Bring to a boil and stir until the cream thickens and curdles slightly. Add the fish sauce and sugar and stir into the curry mixture.

4 Add the fish pieces and stock. Let simmer, stirring occasionally, for 3–4 minutes, or until the fish is just tender. Add the lime leaves and basil, then cook for an additional minute.

5 Transfer to a warmed serving dish and serve with plain boiled rice or noodles.

bouillabaisse

serves six–eight

5 tbsp olive oil

2 large onions, finely chopped

1 leek, finely chopped

4 garlic cloves, crushed

½ small fennel bulb, finely chopped

5 ripe tomatoes, peeled
and chopped

1 fresh thyme sprig

2 strips orange rind

salt and pepper

7 cups hot fish stock

4 lb 8 oz/2 kg mixed seafood, such
as porgy, sea bass, red snapper,
cod, and skate, coarsely
chopped; soft shell crabs, raw
shrimp, and langoustines,
left whole

12–18 thick slices French bread

BELL PEPPER & SAFFRON SAUCE

1 red bell pepper, seeded
and cut into fourths

⅔ cup light olive oil

1 egg yolk

large pinch of saffron threads

pinch of dried red pepper flakes

lemon juice, to taste

salt and pepper

1 Preheat the broiler. To make the sauce, brush the bell pepper pieces with a little of the oil and cook under the hot broiler for 5–6 minutes on each side, or until charred and tender. Remove from the heat and place in a plastic bag until cool enough to handle. Peel the skins away.

2 Place the bell pepper pieces in a food processor with the egg yolk, saffron, pepper flakes, lemon juice, and salt and pepper to taste and process until smooth. Start adding the remaining oil, drop by drop, until the mixture starts to thicken. Continue adding the oil in a steady stream until it is all incorporated and the mixture is thick. Add a little hot water if too thick.

3 In a large pan, heat the oil and add the onions, leek, garlic, and fennel, then cook for 10–15 minutes, or until softened and starting to color. Add the tomatoes, thyme, orange rind, and salt and pepper to taste and cook for an additional 5 minutes, or until the tomatoes have collapsed.

4 Add the stock and bring to a boil. Reduce the heat and let simmer gently for 10 minutes, or until all the vegetables are tender. Add the seafood and return to a boil, then reduce the heat and let simmer for 10 minutes, or until the seafood is tender.

5 When the soup is ready, toast the bread on both sides. Using a slotted spoon, divide the fish between serving plates. Add some of the soup to moisten and serve with the bread. Hand round the sauce to accompany. Serve the remaining soup separately.

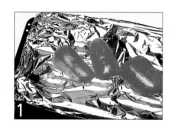

cotriade

serves four

large pinch of saffron threads

2½ cups hot fish stock

1 tbsp olive oil

2 tbsp butter

1 onion, sliced

2 garlic cloves, chopped

1 leek, sliced

1 small fennel bulb, thinly sliced

1 lb/450 g potatoes, cut into chunks

⅔ cup dry white wine

1 tbsp fresh thyme leaves

2 bay leaves

4 ripe tomatoes, peeled
  and chopped

2 lb/900 g mixed fish fillets, such as
  haddock, hake, mackerel, red
  snapper, coarsely chopped

2 tbsp chopped fresh parsley

salt and pepper

crusty bread, to serve

COOK'S TIP

Once the fish and vegetables
have been cooked, you could
process the soup in a food
processor or blender and strain
it to give a smooth fish soup.

---

1 Using a mortar and pestle, crush the saffron and add to the stock. Stir the mixture and set aside to infuse for at least 10 minutes.

2 Heat the oil and butter together in a large, heavy-bottom pan. Add the onion and cook over low heat, stirring occasionally, for 4–5 minutes, or until softened. Add the garlic, leek, fennel, and potatoes. Cover and cook for an additional 10–15 minutes, or until the vegetables are softened.

3 Add the wine and let simmer rapidly for 3–4 minutes, or until reduced by about half. Add the thyme, bay leaves, and tomatoes and stir well. Add the saffron-infused stock. Bring to a boil, then reduce the heat and let simmer gently, covered, for 15 minutes, or until all the vegetables are tender.

4 Add the fish and return to a boil. Reduce the heat and let simmer for an additional 3–4 minutes, or until all the fish is tender. Add the parsley and salt and pepper to taste. Using a slotted spoon, transfer the fish and vegetables to a warmed serving dish. Serve with plenty of crusty bread.

shrimp with tomatoes

serves four–six

3 onions

1 green bell pepper

1 tsp finely chopped fresh
  gingerroot

1 garlic clove, crushed

1 tsp salt

1 tsp chili powder

2 tbsp lemon juice

12 oz/350 g frozen cooked
  shelled shrimp

3 tbsp oil

14 oz/400 g canned tomatoes

chopped fresh cilantro, to garnish

boiled rice and green salad, to serve

COOK'S TIP

Fresh gingerroot looks rather
like a knobbly potato. The
skin should be peeled, then
the flesh either grated, finely
chopped or sliced. Ginger is
also available ground: this can
be used as a substitute for fresh
gingerroot, but the flavor of
the fresh root is far superior.

1 Using a sharp knife, slice the onions and seed and slice the green bell pepper.

2 Place the ginger, garlic, salt, and chili powder in a small bowl and mix to combine. Add the lemon juice and mix to form a paste.

3 Place the shrimp in a bowl of cold water and set aside to thaw. Drain thoroughly.

4 Heat the oil in a medium-size skillet. Add the onions and sauté until golden brown.

5 Add the spice paste to the onions, reduce the heat to low, and cook, stirring and mixing well, for 3 minutes.

6 Add the tomatoes and their juice and the bell pepper, and cook for 5–7 minutes, stirring occasionally.

7 Add the shrimp to the skillet and cook for 10 minutes, stirring occasionally. Garnish with cilantro and serve hot with plain boiled rice and a crisp green salad.

shrimp & tuna pasta bake

serves four

8 oz/225 g tricolor pasta shapes

1 tbsp vegetable oil

1 bunch scallions, chopped

6 oz/175 g white
   mushrooms, sliced

14 oz/400 g canned tuna in brine,
   drained and flaked

6 oz/175 g cooked shelled shrimp,
   thawed if frozen

2 tbsp cornstarch

scant 2 cups skim milk

salt and pepper

4 tomatoes, thinly sliced

½ cup fresh bread crumbs

¼ cup grated Cheddar cheese

TO SERVE

whole-wheat bread

fresh salad

1 Preheat the oven to 375°F/190°C. Bring a large pan of water to the boil and cook the pasta according to the package directions. Drain well.

2 Meanwhile, heat the oil in a skillet and sauté all but a handful of the scallions and all of the mushrooms, stirring, for 4–5 minutes, or until softened.

3 Place the cooked pasta in a bowl and mix in the scallions and mushrooms, tuna, and shrimp. Set aside until required.

4 Blend the cornstarch with a little of the milk to make a paste. Pour the remaining milk into a pan and stir in the paste. Heat, stirring, until the sauce starts to thicken. Season well with salt and pepper.

5 Pour the sauce over the pasta mixture and stir until well combined. Transfer to an ovenproof gratin dish and place on a baking sheet.

6 Arrange the tomato slices over the pasta and sprinkle with the bread crumbs and cheese. Bake in the oven for 25–30 minutes, or until golden. Serve, sprinkled with the reserved scallions and accompanied by bread and salad.

seafood lasagna

serves four

3 tbsp butter, plus extra
   for greasing

generous ¼ cup all-purpose flour

1 tsp mustard powder

2½ cups milk

2 tbsp olive oil

1 onion, chopped

2 garlic cloves, finely chopped

1 tbsp fresh thyme leaves

1 lb/450 g mixed mushrooms, sliced

⅔ cup white wine

14 oz/400 g canned
   chopped tomatoes

salt and pepper

1 lb/450 g mixed skinless white fish
   fillets, cubed

8 oz/225 g shelled scallops, prepared

4–6 sheets fresh lasagna

8 oz/225 g mozzarella cheese,
   drained and chopped

1 Preheat the oven to 400°F/200°C. Melt the butter in a pan. Add the flour and mustard powder and stir until smooth. Cook gently for 2 minutes without coloring. Gradually add the milk, whisking until smooth. Bring to a boil, then reduce the heat and let simmer for 2 minutes. Remove from the heat and set aside. Cover the surface of the sauce with plastic wrap to prevent a skin forming.

2 Heat the oil in a skillet over medium heat and add the onion, garlic, and thyme. Cook for 5 minutes, or until softened. Add the mushrooms and cook for an additional 5 minutes, or until softened. Stir in the wine and boil rapidly until nearly evaporated. Stir in the tomatoes. Bring to a boil, then reduce the heat and let simmer, covered, for 15 minutes. Season to taste with salt and pepper and set aside.

3 Lightly grease a lasagna dish. Spoon half the tomato sauce over the base of the dish and top with half the fish and scallops.

4 Layer half the lasagna over the fish, then pour over half the white sauce and add half the mozzarella. Repeat these layers, finishing with the white sauce and mozzarella.

5 Bake the lasagna in the oven for 35–40 minutes, or until bubbling and golden and the fish is cooked through. Remove from the oven and let stand on a heat-resistant surface or mat for 10 minutes before serving.

seafood spaghetti

serves four

2 tsp olive oil

1 small red onion, finely chopped

1 tbsp lemon juice

1 garlic clove, crushed

2 celery stalks, finely chopped

⅔ cup fish stock

⅔ cup dry white wine

small bunch fresh tarragon

1 lb/450 g live mussels, scrubbed
  and debearded

8 oz/225 g raw shrimp, shelled
  and deveined

8 oz/225 g baby squid, cleaned and
  cut into rings

8 small cooked crab claws, cracked

8 oz/225 g dried spaghetti

salt and pepper

2 tbsp chopped fresh tarragon,
  to garnish

COOK'S TIP

Crab claws contain lean crabmeat. Ask your store to crack the claws for you, leaving the pincers intact, because the shell is very tough.

1 Heat the oil in a large pan and sauté the onion with the lemon juice, garlic, and celery for 3–4 minutes, or until just softened.

2 Pour in the stock and wine. Bring to a boil and add the tarragon and mussels. Reduce the heat and let simmer, covered, for 5 minutes. Add the shrimp, squid, and crab claws to the skillet, then mix together and cook for 3–4 minutes, or until the mussels have opened, the shrimp are pink, and the squid is opaque. Discard the tarragon and any mussels that have not opened.

3 Meanwhile, cook the spaghetti in a pan of boiling water according to the package directions. Drain well.

4 Add the spaghetti to the shellfish mixture and toss together. Season to taste with salt and pepper.

5 Transfer to warmed serving plates and spoon over the cooking juices. Serve garnished with tarragon.

243

sardinian red snapper

generous ¼ cup golden raisins

⅔ cup red wine

2 tbsp olive oil

2 onions, sliced

1 zucchini, cut into 2-inch/
   5-cm sticks

2 oranges

2 tsp coriander seeds,
   lightly crushed

4 red snapper, boned and filleted

1¾ oz/50 g canned anchovies,
   drained

2 tbsp chopped fresh oregano

COOK'S TIP

Red snapper is usually available
all year round—frozen, if not
fresh—from your supermarket.
If you cannot get hold of it, try
using tilapia.
This dish can also be served
warm, if you prefer.

1 Place the golden raisins in a
bowl. Pour over the wine and let
soak for 10 minutes.

2 Heat the oil in a large skillet.
Add the onions and sauté for
2 minutes.

3 Add the zucchini to the skillet and
sauté for an additional 3 minutes,
or until just tender.

4 Using a zester, pare long, thin
strips of rind from one of the
oranges. Using a sharp knife, remove
the skin from both of the oranges,
then segment the oranges by slicing
between the lines of pith.

5 Add the orange rind to the skillet.
Add the wine, golden raisins,
coriander seeds, red snapper, and
anchovies to the skillet and let simmer
for 10–15 minutes, or until the fish is
cooked through.

6 Stir in the oregano and orange
segments, then set aside and let
cool. Place the mixture in a large bowl
and let chill, covered, in the refrigerator
for at least 2 hours so that the flavors
mingle. Transfer to serving plates and
serve at once.

fideua

serves six

3 tbsp olive oil

1 large onion, chopped

2 garlic cloves, finely chopped

pinch of saffron threads, crushed

½ tsp paprika

3 tomatoes, peeled, seeded,
   and chopped

12 oz/350 g dried egg vermicelli,
   broken into 2-inch/5-cm lengths

⅔ cup white wine

1¼ cups fish stock

12 large raw shrimp

18 live mussels, scrubbed
   and debearded

12 oz/350 g cleaned squid, cut
   into rings

18 large live clams, scrubbed

2 tbsp chopped fresh parsley

salt and pepper

lemon wedges, to serve

1 Heat the oil in a large skillet or paella pan. Add the onion and cook over low heat for 5 minutes, or until softened. Add the garlic and cook for an additional 30 seconds. Add the saffron and paprika and stir well. Add the tomatoes and cook for 2–3 minutes until they have collapsed.

VARIATION
Try using langoustines, shrimp, and angler fish for a change.

2 Add the vermicelli and stir well. Add the wine to the skillet and boil rapidly until it has been absorbed.

3 Add the stock, shrimp, mussels, squid, and clams. Stir and return to low simmer for 10 minutes, or until the shrimp and squid are cooked through and the mussels and clams have opened. Discard any that remain shut. The stock should be almost completely absorbed.

4 Add the parsley and season to taste with salt and pepper. Serve at once in warmed bowls, with lemon wedges.

moroccan fish tagine

serves four

2 tbsp olive oil

1 large onion, finely chopped

pinch of saffron threads

½ tsp ground cinnamon

1 tsp ground coriander

½ tsp ground cumin

½ tsp ground turmeric

7 oz/200 g canned
   chopped tomatoes

1¼ cups fish stock

4 small red snapper, boned and
   heads and tails removed

⅓ cup pitted green olives

1 tbsp chopped preserved lemon

3 tbsp chopped cilantro

salt and pepper

cooked couscous, to serve

COOK'S TIP

To preserve lemons, take enough
to fill a preserving jar. Cut into
fourths lengthwise, but do not
cut right through. Pack with 2 oz/
55 g sea salt per lemon. Add the
juice of 1 more lemon and cover
with water. Leave for 1 month.

1 Heat the oil in a large pan or ovenproof casserole over low heat. Add the onion and cook, stirring occasionally, for 10 minutes, or until softened but not colored. Add the saffron, cinnamon, ground coriander, cumin, and turmeric and cook for 30 seconds, stirring.

2 Add the tomatoes and stock and stir well. Bring to a boil, then reduce the heat and let simmer, covered, for 15 minutes. Uncover and let the sauce simmer for an additional 20–35 minutes, or until thickened.

3 Cut each red snapper in half, then add the pieces to the skillet, pushing them into the sauce. Let simmer for an additional 5–6 minutes, or until the fish is just cooked.

4 Carefully stir in the olives, preserved lemon, and the cilantro. Season to taste with salt and pepper and serve with couscous.

celery & salt cod casserole

9 oz/250 g salt cod,
   soaked overnight

1 tbsp oil

4 shallots, finely chopped

2 garlic cloves, chopped

3 celery stalks, chopped

14 oz/400 g canned
   tomatoes, chopped

⅔ cup fish stock

scant ⅓ cup pine nuts

2 tbsp coarsely chopped
   fresh tarragon

2 tbsp capers

crusty bread or mashed potatoes,
   to serve

COOK'S TIP

Salt cod is a useful ingredient to
keep in the pantry and, once
soaked, can be used in the same
way as any other fish. It does,
however, have a stronger flavor
than normal, and it is, of course,
slightly salty. It can be found in
larger supermarkets and
delicatessens.

1 Drain the salt cod, then rinse it under plenty of cold running water and drain again thoroughly. Remove and discard any skin and bones. Pat the fish dry with paper towels and then cut it into chunks.

2 Heat the oil in a large skillet. Add the shallots and garlic and cook for 2–3 minutes. Add the celery and cook for an additional 2 minutes, then add the tomatoes and stock.

3 Bring the mixture to a boil, then reduce the heat and let simmer for 5 minutes.

4 Add the fish and cook for 10 minutes, or until tender.

5 Meanwhile, preheat the broiler. Place the pine nuts on a baking sheet. Place under the hot broiler and toast for 2–3 minutes, or until golden.

6 Stir the tarragon, capers, and pine nuts into the fish casserole and heat gently to warm through.

7 Transfer to serving plates and serve with fresh crusty bread or mashed potatoes.

spanish fish stew

serves four

5 tbsp olive oil

2 large onions, finely chopped

2 tomatoes, peeled, seeded, and diced

2 slices white bread, crusts removed

4 almonds, toasted

3 garlic cloves, coarsely chopped

12 oz/350 g cooked lobster

7 oz/200 g cleaned squid

7 oz/200 g angler fish fillet

7 oz/200 g cod fillet, skinned

salt and pepper

1 tbsp all-purpose flour

6 large raw shrimp

6 langoustines

18 live mussels, scrubbed and debearded

8 large live clams, scrubbed

1 tbsp chopped fresh parsley

½ cup brandy

1 Heat 3 tablespoons of the oil in a skillet over medium heat and cook the onions for 10–15 minutes, or until lightly golden. Add the tomatoes and cook until they have collapsed. Set aside.

2 Heat 1 tablespoon of the remaining oil in a skillet and sauté the bread until crisp. Break into pieces and put into a mortar with the almonds and 2 garlic cloves. Pound to a fine paste with a pestle. Alternatively, process in a food processor.

3 Split the lobster lengthwise. Remove and discard the intestinal vein, the stomach sac, and the spongy gills. Crack the claws and remove the meat. Take out the flesh from the tail and chop into large chunks. Slice the squid into rings.

4 Season the angler fish, cod, and lobster to taste with salt and pepper and dust with flour. Heat a little of the remaining oil in an ovenproof casserole and separately brown the angler fish, cod, lobster, squid, shrimp, and langoustines. Then return all the fish to the casserole.

5 Add the mussels and clams and the remaining garlic and parsley. Set the casserole over low heat. Pour over the brandy and ignite. When the flames have died down, add the tomato mixture and just enough water to cover. Bring to a boil, then let simmer for 3–4 minutes, or until the mussels and clams have opened. Stir in the bread mixture and season. Let simmer for a few minutes, then serve.

cuttlefish in their own ink

serves four

1 lb/450 g small cuttlefish, with
their ink sacs

4 tbsp olive oil

1 small onion, finely chopped

2 garlic cloves, finely chopped

1 tsp paprika

6 oz/175 g ripe tomatoes, peeled,
seeded, and chopped

⅔ cup red wine

⅔ cup fish stock

salt and pepper

1½ cups instant cornmeal

3 tbsp chopped fresh
flatleaf parsley

1 Cut off the cuttlefish tentacles
in front of the eyes and remove
the beak from the center of the
tentacles. Cut the head from the body
and discard. Cut open the body section
along the dark-colored back. Remove
the cuttle bone and the entrails,
reserving the ink sac. Skin the body.
Chop the flesh coarsely and set aside.
Split open the ink sac and dilute the
ink in a little water. Set aside.

2 Heat the oil in a large pan over
medium heat, then add the onion
and cook for 8–10 minutes, or until
softened and golden. Add the garlic
and cook for an additional 30 seconds.
Add the cuttlefish and cook for an
additional 5 minutes, or until starting
to brown. Add the paprika and stir for
30 seconds before adding the
tomatoes. Cook for 2–3 minutes,
or until collapsed.

3 Add the wine, stock, and diluted
ink and stir well. Bring to a boil,
then let simmer gently, uncovered, for
25 minutes, or until the cuttlefish is
tender and the sauce has thickened.
Season to taste with salt and pepper.

4 Meanwhile, cook the cornmeal
according to the package
directions. When cooked, remove from
the heat and stir in the parsley and salt
and pepper to taste.

5 Divide the cornmeal between
plates and top with the cuttlefish
and its sauce.

luxury fish pie

serves four

3 oz/85 g butter

3 shallots, finely chopped

4 oz/115 g mushrooms, halved

2 tbsp dry white wine

2 lb/900 g live mussels, scrubbed
and debearded

2½ cups fish stock

10½ oz/300 g angler fish fillet,
cubed

10½ oz/300 g skinless
cod fillet, cubed

10½ oz/300 g skinless lemon sole
fillet, cubed

4 oz/115 g raw jumbo shrimp,
shelled and deveined

2 tbsp all-purpose flour

¼ cup heavy cream

salt and pepper

fresh parsley sprigs, to garnish

POTATO TOPPING

3 lb 5 oz/1.5 kg mealy potatoes,
cut into chunks

3 tbsp butter

2 egg yolks

½ cup milk

pinch of freshly grated nutmeg

salt and pepper

1 Preheat the oven to 400°F/200°C. For the filling, melt 2 tbsp of the butter in a skillet, then add the shallots and cook for 5 minutes, or until softened. Add the mushrooms and cook over high heat for 2 minutes. Add the wine and let simmer until the liquid has evaporated. Transfer to a 6-cup shallow ovenproof dish and set aside.

2 Put the mussels into a large pan with just the water clinging to their shells and cook, covered, over high heat for 3–4 minutes, or until all the mussels have opened. Discard any that remain closed. Drain, reserving the cooking liquid. When cool enough to handle, remove the mussels from their shells and add to the mushrooms.

3 Bring the stock to a boil in a large pan and add the angler fish. Poach gently for 2 minutes before adding the cod, sole, and shrimp. Poach for an additional 2 minutes. Remove the seafood with a slotted spoon and add to the mussels and mushrooms.

4 Melt the remaining butter in a pan and add the flour. Stir until smooth and cook for 2 minutes without coloring. Gradually stir in the hot stock and mussel cooking liquid until smooth and thickened. Add the cream and let simmer gently for 15 minutes, stirring. Season to taste with salt and pepper and pour over the seafood.

5 Meanwhile, make the topping. Boil the potatoes in plenty of salted water for 15–20 minutes, or until tender. Drain well and mash with the butter, egg yolks, milk, nutmeg, and salt and pepper to taste. Pipe or spread over the seafood and roughen the surface of the topping with a fork.

6 Bake in the oven for 30 minutes, until golden and bubbling. Serve straight from the oven, piping hot, garnished with parsley sprigs.